THE GOING DOWN
of the
SONS

CONTENTS

But each one, man for man, has won imperishable praise, each has gained a glorious grave, not that sepulchre of earth wherein they lie, but the living tomb of everlasting remembrance wherein their glory is enshrined, for the whole earth is the sepulchre of heroes.

Monuments may rise and tablets be set up to them in their own land, that no pen or chisel has traced. It is graven, not on stone, but on the living heart of humanity.

Take these men as your example; like them, remember that posterity can only be for the free, that freedom is the sure possession of those alone who have the courage to defend it.

From the Funeral Oration of Pericles (BC 429)

This book is dedicated to those sons who, long ago, in the fields described in this book, fell at the first hurdle of their race for life.

FOREWORD

PROFESSOR CARL CHINN MBE

It was a ritual in our house. Each Remembrance Sunday we would sit before the television with Our Mom and Dad and watch the laying of wreaths at the Cenotaph. It was and is a momentous and moving occasion. Dad always told of us of how proud we should be of the men and women who took part. They had been ready to die for the right to be English and the freedoms that we had we owed to them. They had paid a heavy price. Many, too many, bore the physical wounds of war. Some were blind, others were in wheelchairs, and all of them must have been scarred emotionally and mentally by their experiences.

In those days of my childhood in the early 1960s the veterans of the Second World War were yet middle-aged and there were still large numbers of men honouring their fallen comrades in the First World War. Each year their numbers shrank, but these men who had given their all in the 'war to end all wars' always seemed to arouse a special response from the thousands lining the route of the march past.

When the ceremony was finished, our Dad would fetch out an old cigar tin and open it. Inside were the medals awarded to my Grandad Chinn for his service in the First World War. Dad would take them out and show them to us. There was also a newspaper cutting describing the heroism of Lance Corporal Michael O'Leary. An Irish Guardsman, he won the Victoria Cross by killing all the men on a German machine gun unit in an attack by the Irish Guards and Coldstream Guards at the brickfields of La Bassé on 1st February 1915. My Grandad was in that attack and witnessed Michael O'Leary's bravery.

I was nine when my Grandad died in 1965. I recall sitting on his lap and him telling me of having to eat spiders in the trenches and of how he had fought with the Gurkhas. He used to say one German kept on putting his head above the parapet and would laugh and mock at the Gurkhas, saying that the Gurkhas could not get him with their kukri knives. Then one day the Gurkha soldier told the German to shake his head – and it fell off, because the Gurkha had cut it off without the German knowing.

These were stories told for a young boy and I wished that Grandad had lived long enough to tell the older boy and young man what he had really gone through in that terrible war, of how he had felt and of what he had seen and done. Years later Dad fetched out my Grandad's letters back home to his Mom and I was able to piece together an outline of his involvement, but then and now I wished I knew more.

My Grandad, Private Richard Alfred Chinn number 9968, 2nd Battalion Coldstream Guards, was an Old Contemptible – one of the men who went out with the British Expeditionary Force that went to France in August 1914. Like so many of those from poor neighbourhoods he was a patriot and ended his first letter with 'England for ever'. Grandad fought at the Battle of the Aisne and wrote he would shake hands with himself if he got back in England. Then he was in action at the bloody and bitter 1st Battle of Ypres, where his 'arms ached through shooting so much and quick' in repulsing one German attack.

Soon after the 1st Battle of Ypres, Our Grandad was put in the machine gun section of his battalion. He often asked his Mom if his dad, another Coldstream Guardsman, was proud of his old regiment, and he always wanted to know how the Villa and Blues were doing. Grandad let them know about the heavy rain and mud, and in a letter after Christmas 1915 he emphasised that unlike in some places on the Front there had been no truce with the Germans because 'we were the Guards Brigade where we was out to fight not to play with them as they have found'. Then sometime in February, Grandad was wounded badly in the knee joint at the brickfields at La Bassé. After months of medical treatment and convalescence he was invalided out of the Army.

I hope to visit Flanders and follow in my Grandad's footsteps. I shall take with me The Going Down of the Sons. The sensitive and intuitive poetry of Paul Thornber melded with the expertise and understanding of Terry Carter make this a vital book for anyone, like me, who wants to try and feel what it was like and to know what happened. I can pay no greater tribute to these two men than this: through the power of their words they have truly honoured the Sons of England.

Professor Carl Chinn MBE

THE AUTHORS

PAUL THORNBER

Paul Thornber was born on the 2nd April 1945 in Erdington, Birmingham, was educated at St Philips Grammar School and, at the end of his education, was looked on as something of an educational misfit, in that the range of his six GCE passes did not fit the criteria of any of the professions of the 1960's. This resulted in an occupational history as varied as shells on the shore!

His constant sources of help, inspiration and influence are his wife Elaine, his daughter Louise, and his son Matthew, who have stood by and wondered at some of the strange schemes that Paul has been associated with; wondered, but always supported, knowing that, more often than not, his schemes and ideas would usually be successful. Paul, for his part, looks on these three people as "his finest achievements to date".

His son and daughter have, in turn, married and presented him with four grandchildren. Paul looks on these as "fine results of fine achievements".

Paul is a plain speaker, who does not easily subscribe to social pleasantries. He abhors waste of any kind – time, talent or life – this view is reflected in his poetry.

On reading them, it is clear that imagination plays a large part and, by his own admission, he is mainly interested in attempting to portray feelings and states of mind, "snapshots of the soul" as he calls them.

He has no shortage of ideas, many of which he has not yet fully explored, but one area on which he will not compromise, in his haste to commit thought to paper, is rhyme. He sees this as his ultimate challenge, and spends many hours in its pursuit.

The poetry in this volume, written as a result of many visits to the battlefields of the Somme, is the result of those hours and complements his previous work, "Front Lines", a slim anthology of poetry reflecting general aspects of the First World War. As a result of significant interest in this volume and of his own desire to explore further this period of history, he now feels compelled to return regularly to the scene of the greatest devastation and loss of this tragic period, the Somme battlefields.

His journeys began 11 years ago. He says, "Up 'til that point I, like the great majority, had but a passing interest in the Great War, rekindled for the obligatory two minutes on 11th November each year and marginally heightened by anniversaries of Passchendaele, the Somme, and all those other places and dates which belong to yesteryear, then came the 26th March 1995. This was the beginning of what, for me, have been humbling and harrowing journeys back into those bygone times. Journeys which have seen me visit battlefields in Belgium and France and now the Somme, where the scale of the loss of life, relative to the area covered, has filled me with sadness which, at times, becomes almost too much to bear. My only relief is to commit my thoughts to poetry as I have done within these pages. My journey to this point started in Tyne Cott Cemetery 11 years ago. Those years have been spent in my writing, culminating in this book containing 31 thoughts and poems which evolved from my visits to this area. Each carries a different message. Their sincerity was for me to incorporate, their quality is for you, the reader to judge. My book is a small gesture among many, far more grandiose. It is my voice calling across the ages, crying out my heartfelt thanks to those who, unlike you and I, did not have the chance to reach the end of their journey into life."

TERRY CARTER

Terry Carter was born in Birmingham in 1953 and now lives in Castle Bromwich with his wife and three children.

He says, "I have always had an interest in local history, but my serious interest in the First World War started in 1971 when I bought and read 'The First Day on the Somme', by Martin Middlebrook. As most people do. I began to find out about my own family's involvement. Both my grandfathers survived the war. Isaac Carter served in the Oxford and Bucks Light Infantry in Mesopotamia and Jack Holyoak served in the Royal Field Artillery in Flanders. When I was growing up in the fifties, Jack was a mysterious figure to me. His bedroom was always locked and he spent most of his final years in and out of hospital and convalescent homes. This I later found out was due to a dose of gas poisoning in 1918.

Jack Holyoak was not my grandmother's first husband either. Her first marriage was to Benjamin Gibbons. He had served throughout the war with the Army Service Corps until transferring to a "Quarry Company" of the Royal Engineers. We do not know the full story, but he died of 'Spanish Flu' in April, 1919, whilst home in Birmingham. He is buried in Yardley Cemetery, Birmingham and has a C.W.G.C. headstone. My Nan's two elder brothers, Charlie and Jack Witsey, both died of wounds. Charlie was in the 1st Worcesters, was wounded at the

Somme in November 1916 and died in a military hospital at Etaples, France, whilst Jack served in the 1/5th South Staffs and died of wounds in August 1918. He is buried in Fouquieres Churchyard Extension, near Bruay in France.

My first visit to the former battlefields was not made until October 1991. Accompanied by my brother Chris, and my son Tom, we spent a few days at Ovillers la Boisselle. Our very first stop, and my own very first visit to a Commonwealth War Graves Cemetery, occurred at London Cemetery opposite High Wood. Since then I have made many tips to the former battlefields of France and Belgium. However my main interest lies in the Somme Battlefield and the actions that the Royal Warwickshire Regiment took part in.

When I visit a cemetery or memorial I am always with a group of friends. There is usually a reason why we choose a particular cemetery to visit; it may be a family connection, a Victoria Cross winner is buried there, or perhaps some poor chap that has been "shot at dawn". Because we are on a weekend visit and time is precious, we usually have an itinerary of the places we are going to see and allow ourselves a certain amount of time at each stop. However, what always seems to happen is that, after congregating around the particular headstone, we all seem to meander off in different directions to look at other graves within the cemetery.

Walking along the rows of white headstones in these beautifully maintained cemeteries you lose all sense of time, becoming totally immersed in names, ages, regiments, dates of death and the poignant little inscriptions on the bottom of some headstones chosen by their loved ones. I have to admit, I get lost for words.

In October 2001, Paul and I, together with a few other friends, visited the Somme. This was Paul's second visit to the former battlefields. We walked alongside fields where men had gone "over the top" and been cut down in their hundreds by shot and shell. We visited the cemeteries, the tragic legacy of these actions and the Thiepval memorial commemorating those whose bodies were never found. It was a weekend of mixed emotions; a group of guys one minute laughing and joking; the next quietly walking around a cemetery lost in our own thoughts among the countless headstones.

I feel very privileged Paul has asked me to join him in the production of this book and hope that it will create, in the reader, the desire to keep the memory of those whose lives and deaths are recounted in these pages alive. If the book achieves this, our efforts will have been worthwhile".

1

BEGINNING THE JOURNEY

Since my interest in the First World War was kindled in 1995, on a trip to Ypres, it has now ignited into an all engulfing flame due to my, now frequent, visits to that area of Picardy, which was the scene of such carnage in 1916 and thereafter; the area known as the Somme Battlefields.

I was first introduced to this area by my good friend and co-author of this book, Terry Carter. I had joined the Birmingham Branch of the Western Front Association, and there I met this renowned author of "Birmingham Pals" who, I found out, was a near neighbour and who, by way of a bonus, organised trips, for any interested parties, to the Somme area, which was his abiding interest.

These are not luxury tours, we are all working men, and do not have unlimited leisure time. They usually consist of a mini coach or car journey, starting at 3.00am on Friday mornings, to catch the 8.30am Channel ferry at Dover. The drive from Calais to Auchonvillers, where we usually stay, takes one and a half hours, meaning that we arrive at around midday. This gives us a half day on Friday and a full day on Saturday to walk the paths and fields in good company. These "no frills" excursions are informative, interesting, and above all cheap, which means they can be repeated often!

Terry, and my fellow travellers on these excursions, are most knowledgeable about the events which took place all those years ago. Each has his own special interest. Mine is to try and understand how those brave men and women might have been feeling, faced with the horrors that this area presented to them. These thoughts paved the way for this book which seeks to illustrate their progress through these, now silent, fields in thoughts and poetry.

You could never have known what you were starting those years ago, Terry, but I hope you like the end result! Thanks for your company, friendship and support during my struggle to write this book and on the walks we took together which created it.

These walks usually consist of a six or seven mile hike, along the borders of fields shown in the accompanying aerial photographs of the Somme battlefield area.

The original idea which I had, was to attempt to recreate the feelings, in poetry, of those who walked this way before in 1916. Their arrival, moving up into the line, their life in the front line and their fears when going into action, coupled with their reaction to the horrors they experienced which would, of course, have included seeing their comrades killed, in addition to living with the knowledge, every day, that it might be their turn next. This imaginary journey commences with some general thoughts relating to our group's arrival in the area and is completed by a section containing my own thoughts on the aftermath of the horrific experiences, which were ever present to our predecessors.

In order to help a reader who may feel, as a result of reading this book, that they would like to visit this evocative area of France, I will now give a brief overview of the actions which took place here, the casualties and the cemeteries where the dead were laid to rest. I have also added a map indicating the major towns and cemeteries to help them find their way. By doing this, I hope that they may gain a better understanding of what I am trying to achieve in my writing and, in so doing, gain greater enjoyment of it.

The 1916 Allied offensive on the Western Front was planned as an equal Commonwealth-French effort, to take place on the Somme – until then a relatively quiet sector – where the two armies joined. But, with the French distracted by a major German attack on Verdun to the south, a greater share of the burden fell to the Commonwealth force than was originally intended.

14 divisions, entirely British with the exception of the Newfoundland Regiment, were to launch the offensive on a 23km front between Serre and Maricourt, with a diversionary attack to the north at Gommecourt. The French would go forward on a 13km front to the south.

The 1st July 1916, the first day of what is now known as the Battle of the Somme, was to prove the most catastrophic day's fighting in the history of the British army. Losses were appalling: of the 120,000 British soldiers who fought that day, almost half became casualties, over 19,000 of them dead. 60% of the officers involved were killed, Of the 143 battalions that took part – about half of them 'pals' battalions of the New Army seeing their first action – 32 lost 500 men or more. The Newfoundlanders suffered 70% casualties in just 30 minutes. This was a shockingly high price to pay for the modest gains made at the southern end of the British front. In most places the attack faltered and failed altogether.

With no breakthrough the Battle of the Somme quickly spiralled into the grim, protracted struggle that typified so much of the fighting on the Western Front, drawing in forces from all over the Commonwealth. After that first disastrous day the main effort was concentrated in a push north and east from the southern sector. A surprise night attack (including a rare First World War cavalry charge made by the Indian Cavalry Division) captured most of the Bazentin-Longueval ridge on 14th July but the Germans could not be moved out of High Wood and Delville Wood where the South African Brigade was badly mauled.

In early August Poziéres ridge fell to the Australians after two weeks bitter fighting but progress in the weeks that followed was slow and uneven, with stubborn German resistance meaning a major fight for every copse, farm and village.

On 15th September the offensive was given fresh impetus when tanks made their first appearance on the battlefield and the line was pushed on toward Courcelette, Martinpuich and Flers. Thiepval finally fell on 26th September. The slow forward advance continued through October as the weather deteriorated and when the fighting was finally called to a halt in mid-November, after a last effort that finally took Beaumont Hamel, the Commonwealth had suffered almost 420,000 casualties, 125,000 of them dead. The French to the south had lost more than 200,000. In places the line had been pushed forward 11 to 13km; elsewhere it had not moved at all.

A few months later, in the spring of 1917, the Germans made a tactical withdrawal to the heavily fortified Hindenburg Line giving up an area more than 10 times greater than that hard won by the Allies the previous summer.

Today the evidence of what happened there in the summer of 1916 is impossible to miss. Though restored to its rural tranquillity, the chalky landscape still bears the scars of trench systems, mines and colossal bombardment. Villages and farms devastated by shelling and now rebuilt look startlingly new. The area is thick with memorials marking military exploits. And, of course, there are the many cemeteries.

In the area covered by the Somme battlefields alone, some 150,000 Commonwealth servicemen (50,000 of them unidentified) lie buried in 250 military and 150 civilian cemeteries. Six memorials to the missing commemorate by name more than 100,000 whose graves are not known.

Commonwealth forces served on the Somme front from July 1915 and suffered greatly there in 1918 during the great German breakthrough, but almost half of the identified burials and 80% of the missing relate to just 20 weeks' fighting in 1916.

The cemeteries and memorials, constructed by the Imperial (later Commonwealth) War Graves Commission in the years after the war, stand primarily as permanent monuments to the men who fought and died there, but they also say much about the 1916 battle, the way it was fought, and the monumental task of accounting for the dead that continued long after the war was over. They show what went on in the rear areas, they tell us who fought where and when, the units involved in the big pushes and when they happened, where the line moved and where it stood still. They speak of small incidents and large, disaster and success, the aftermath and the appalling cost in human life. Each cemetery, each memorial to the missing contributes its own part to the story of the Somme. Each has its own history.

The battlefield itself was dotted with hundreds of tiny cemeteries where men had been hastily buried by their comrades where they fell. But the nature of much of the 1916 battle - constant attacks and counter-attacks, little or no forward movement - left thousands dead in No Man's Land. Their bodies could not be recovered while the fighting continued and the ceaseless pounding of artillery meant many were lost for good.

In 1917, with the devastated battlefield in Allied hands, the work of bringing in and burying the dead was begun by the British V Corps. This created many new cemeteries. Battlefield clearance resumed in earnest after the Armistice and the area was swept at least six times in the search for bodies. As time went on, fewer and fewer could be identified - this was before the introduction of durable identity tags - and the many new and vast 'concentration' cemeteries filled up with ranks of the unknown. The last of these cemeteries was declared complete in 1934, but by the outbreak of the Second World War a further 3,000 bodies had been found and discoveries continue even today.

The names of the thousands of dead from the battle whose bodies were not recovered or identified were inscribed on memorials to the missing, the Australians and Canadians on their national memorials at Villers-Bretonneux and Vimy, the rest on memorials on the old battlefield itself. The largest, the Thiepval Memorial, carries more than 72,000 names.

The cemeteries of the Somme will give up their stories if the visitor knows what to look for. In all but the smallest cemeteries there will be a register usually found in a bronze locker near the entrance or in one of the shelter buildings - listing all of the dead buried in the cemetery. The register also contains a historical note, giving a few details of what went on in the immediate area during the battle and how the cemetery was made, and a cemetery plan showing the layout of the plots and rows.

As well as personal details, the headstones of the identified dead carry national, regimental or unit information and dates of death. Special memorial headstones, usually arranged in groups or around the cemetery boundary, commemorate men whose known graves in a particular cemetery could not be found, perhaps because the cemetery was damaged in later fighting, or the temporary grave marker lost.

But it is the graves of the unknown that characterise many of the Somme cemeteries. If partial identification was possible - rank, regiment or unit - this is given on the headstone. By far the most, those of the entirely unidentified, simply bear the inscription "A Soldier of the Great War, Known unto God."

Of the Commonwealth dead lost during the 1916 Battle of the Somme, almost 77,000 were denied the honour of a known grave. The national memorials at Vimy and Villers-Bretonneux commemorate more than 4,500 Canadians and 5,000 Australians who died between July and November 1916. The fierce fighting of September and October alone cost the New Zealand Division more than 1,500 men of whom a staggering 1,200 have no known grave. They are commemorated on a memorial at Caterpillar Valley Cemetery, the second largest cemetery on the Somme, at the heart of the battlefield where they lost their lives. The Royal Newfoundland Regiment's close links with the battlefield at Beaumont-Hamel led to the creation of the memorial park there after the war and the memorial to the missing of Newfoundland, surmounted by a great Caribou, lists 200 lost on the Somme. But by far the majority of the Somme's missing, the 840 South African and 65,000 British who died during the months of battle and have no known grave, are commemorated on the huge, imposing memorial at Thiepval.

This 45 metre high memorial stands on an open ridge just south of Thiepval village and can be seen on the skyline from many parts of the battlefield. The design by Sir Edwin Lutyens, is a massive stepped arrangement of intersecting arches that culminate in a towering central arch 24 metres high. Clad in brick, the memorial's 16 piers are faced with Portland stone on which the names of the dead are engraved.

The Thiepval Memorial is both memorial to the missing and battle memorial commemorating the joint Commonwealth-French offensive of 1916 and a cemetery with equal numbers of Commonwealth and French graves, gathered together from all over the battlefield, is laid out in front.

From this short pen picture of the enormity of the tragedy and casualties sustained in this small area of Picardy, and my brief introduction to the many memorials and cemeteries which proliferate there, I hope you will have gained an insight into why I have to keep returning to this terrible, yet beautiful part of France. Each visit brings new inspiration, each walk evokes new thoughts, questions and eventually, poems.

Join Terry and me on this, our latest, journey. We appreciate your company and hope that, at its end, you will come to understand, through my poetry, and Terry's most interesting background notes, more about this tragic, evocative, area which was the scene of the "Going Down of the Sons".

Paul J Thornber

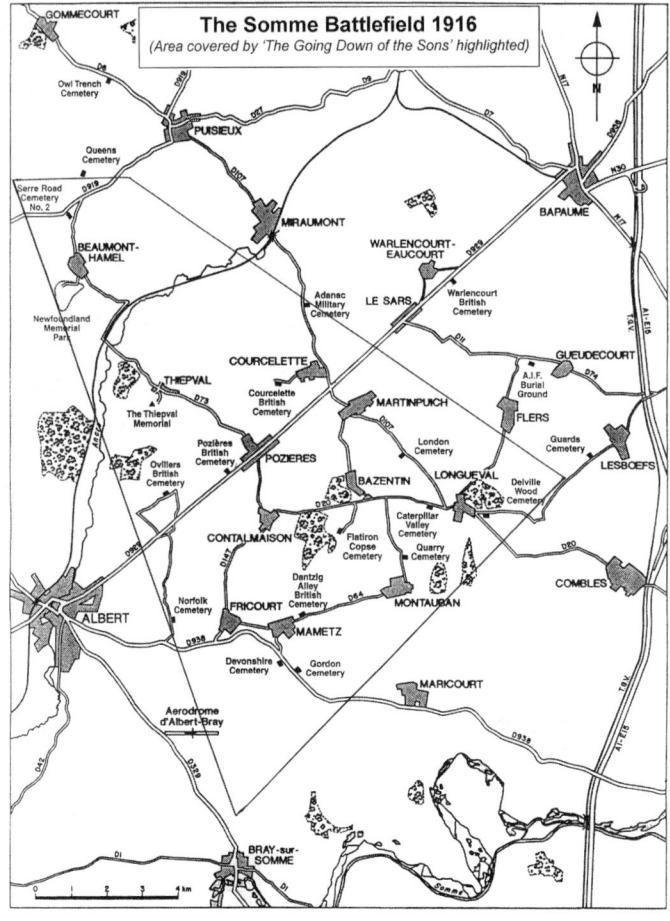

MAMETZ WOOD AND HAPPY VALLEY

THIEPVAL

CONTALMAISON

NEWFOUNDLAND PARK

SCHWABEN REDOUBT

DELVILLE WOOD

FLATIRON COPSE

HIGH WOOD

2

VISITING

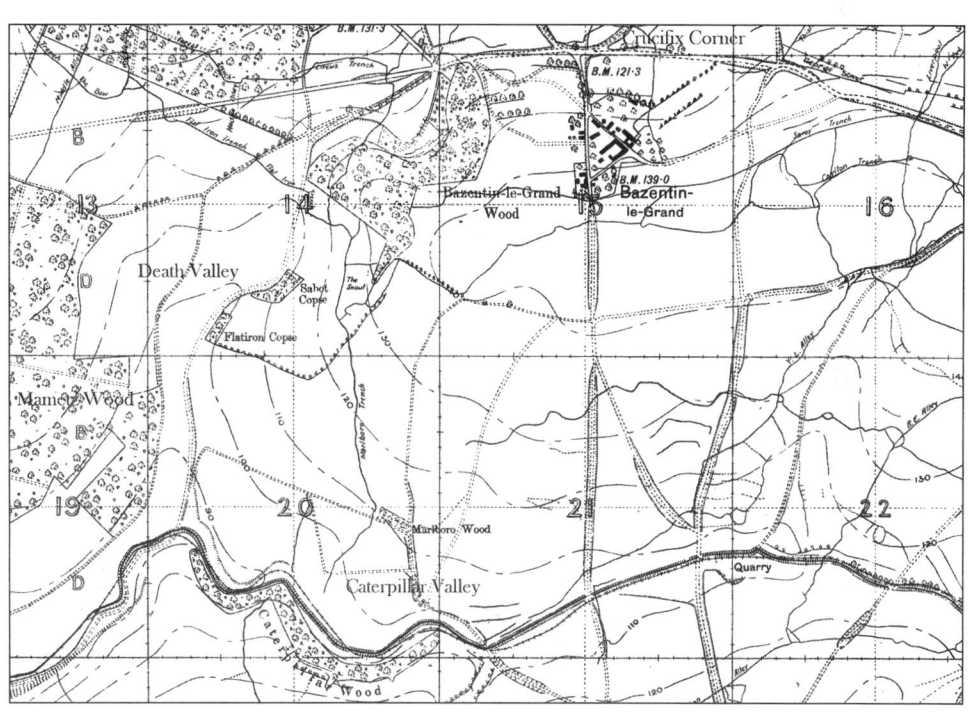

THE CELLAR

My friends and I frequently stay at Avril Williams' guest house in Auchonvillers. Avril is an emigrant from Nailsworth, Gloucestershire of some 14 years' residence In France. She really has a feel for what went on in this area, and is more than prepared to share information with anyone who is interested, but what I really like about her is, she is a genuine lady who doesn't suffer fools gladly.

The added attraction of staying with her is that, although all the properties in the area were destroyed in the Great War, her guest house is built on a cellar which survived it.

This cellar was used as a dressing station, and prison and the Imperial War Museum are currently working with Avril to excavate and restore the support trenches which supplied it.

Avril will, on request, give a candlelit tour and talk in the cellar which is highly evocative and partially recreates conditions as they must have been all those years ago. The cellar experience is further enhanced by some of the names of the previous occupants being carved on its walls and, during Avril's, talk it is easy to let your mind drift back over the years to the time when these cellars were occupied by those whose names are still visible.

Many theme parks have recently sprung up trying to recreate events of yesterday. Avril's tour and talk easily achieve this with no artificial props. Is it any wonder, then, that such a place inspired this poem?

THE CELLAR

Stop upon your journey pilgrim, step down into hallowed ground,
Walk in catacombs of memory, yesteryear is all around,
Footsteps of the brave, the fearful and the saints who healed the pain,
Lost in time, now rediscovered, bearing mute witness again
To a time, free from the madness, brief respite from out the fray,
Some who lingered gone forever, some would see another day.

Let the atmosphere surround you, bygone echoes, whispered calls,
History is all around you, in the writing on the walls,
Names known in a bygone era, children safe within this womb,
Long forgotten, now remembered by their shadows in the gloom,
Here in darkness, hear the voice of reason as their tale is told
And remember, in its telling, those who will never grow old.

FIVE NEW FRIENDS

It is always rewarding that, when we go to the Somme, everyone, even if we have never met before, gets on well. I guess this is because, even though we all have our specific areas of interest, we all share a common bond, that of respect and empathy for the events which took place in the area.

Five of us were lucky enough to be present at the site of the German strongpoint, the Heidenkopf Redoubt, or Quadrilateral on the Serre Road when it was being excavated in order to make the TV programme "Ancestors" about Wilfred Owen, the war poet, who briefly occupied a dugout within it in 1917 during British occupation.

Three bodies, two German and one British, were unearthed during the exercise, proof that the Somme still gives up its dead, even after 90 years!

It was a privilege to see, at first hand, the work of the archaeologists and to also see, unearthed for the first time, the duckboards in the bottom of the trench. We were also very interested in various artefacts which had been discovered. These included sniper plates and the largest shell I have yet seen. This was removed from site at the earliest opportunity, but not before we had photographed it! This was a once in a lifetime experience and one which I will long remember, hence this poem.

FIVE NEW FRIENDS

Before the faithful congregated, in their Sunday act of praise,
Five new friends silently gathered in the early morning haze,
Shrouded in the mists of autumn, ere the sun was raised aloft,
Five friends looked through history's window, on rediscovered Heidenkopf.

Like a gash in earth still sleeping, to the heavens now laid bare,
Excavated and uncovered, five friends now saw what first lay there,
Five friends stood and gazed in wonder, through the years, at yesterday,
All must soon be covered over, what lies here, lies here to stay.

Duckboards reappear before them, history's surviving piers
Disappear into the tunnels, silent sepulchres of years,
Facing outward, ever onward, on to undermine the foe,
Ground once taken, then recovered, no man's land of long ago.

Wooden crosses, laid on chalk, mark brave men's passing from their woe,
Resurrected, duly honoured, for three lives not much to show,
But five new friends have seen this place, and five new friends would all agree
Their souls rest with other legions, in those five friends' memory.

THE BAYONET

One of the greatest pleasures I have, is walking the ploughed fields of Picardy after harvest time, in company with good friends, visualising, thanks to Terry's commentary, the events that took place so long ago and, whilst being mindful that many of those who fell, in conflict, are still at rest beneath the chalky soil, I cannot escape the thrill of finding newly uncovered remnants of those times on the surface.

Usually, it is shrapnel balls, spent bullets and occasionally more dangerous remnants of unexploded ordnances, which are treated with due respect and set aside for later disposal. Occasionally, more personal items are found; a tunic button, a cap badge and, on one occasion, a family staying at Avril's guest house with us found a bayonet, almost complete, long buried and forgotten in the turmoil of war. This find inspired this poem. That bayonet may have accompanied its owner for years, may have tasted blood, but how was it separated from its owner? Who was he? What happened to him? I don't know the answers, but these are the kind of questions that walking these fields, so steeped in history, bring to my mind.

THE BAYONET

My friend, for so long have I carried you about
You are no longer heavy, yet weight of our kills
Hangs over me, and sows shadowy seeds of doubt,
Who will be final victor in this clash of wills?

You who have known no fear, yet steeped in blood
Accompanies me in every round of this great fight,
Not caring if the reason for our strife is good,
Confident in the knowledge, "it is right".

And any call for mercy would be vain indeed,
For enemy to enemy can never speak
And foe may never cry for help, nor plead,
Only the strong can overcome the weak.

When all is done and dead fall high upon the dead,
Covering these fields within this foreign land
With poppies, in an endless carpet of blood red,
I look to you and you are still to hand.

So let them try to separate us if they dare,
When all is done, we look upon their failure with scorn,
We are inseparable, by all the deaths we share
And I will keep you close, my English thorn.

SUNBATHING

The battlefields of the Somme are, in a strange way, beautiful. They are the sleeping place of so many and like an eiderdown, the green fields are covered with poppies, the accepted symbol of remembrance. It is known that these flowers only grow on disturbed ground and no ground in Europe was ever more disturbed! Walking the fields when these are on display is most moving as, even now, they return, year after year, to mark the places of dying. Some fields contain strips of poppies which look, against the green, like reddened, raw slashes on the skin of Picardy.

I wrote this poem one afternoon when I "immersed myself in war" in fields at the side of the Mametz Wood. It is so easy to let the mind return over the years and try to visualise, in my mind's eye, the feelings of those who passed by and those of the many who remain here still.

I am no historian or battle expert, but I walk with those who are. Terry and the rest of my friends have the ability to provide a backdrop for my thoughts, by describing what happened those years ago and when you have a backdrop, a stage and a script, you have a theatre. The original actors are no more but, in theatres such as these, they are never far from my thoughts.

SUNBATHING

Pale sabre slashes gape where once was green,
And in the wounds sparse poppies rise embarrassed, faces red,
The smiling sun shines down upon a summer scene
Where late alive now lie still, dull, and dead
And in the sky the sad and sleepy clouds slide by
Hiding from ugliness where beauty thrived before,
In midst of life we are in death, here was the place to die,
My life suspended, I immerse myself in war.

"THE LITTLE CHAP"

One Saturday afternoon, whilst walking in Caterpillar Valley, I came across Flatiron Copse Cemetery in which, at plot 3, row J, grave 3 is buried Corporal Edward Dwyer VC.

Edward was a regular soldier at the outbreak of the Great War, during which he won his VC at Hill 60, Belgium on the 21st April 1915. The War Office recalled him to England, where they used this modest young man's exemplary service record to encourage others to enlist. They did this by making one of the earliest propaganda recordings, still available on the CD "Oh, It's a Lovely War".

He was below average height at 5ft 3 inches, describing himself as "a very little chap". Being wounded whilst winning his VC he was repatriated, returning to his battalion in France in early 1916. He was promoted to Corporal on the 27th July 1916 and was killed on the 3rd September 1916, leading his men in attack near Guillemont. Having heard Corporal Dwyer's voice across the decades, you may well imagine what a moving experience it was to find his grave. As I knelt beside it, I had the idea for this poem. It was as if the decades had been spanned by the sound of his voice. I had heard him and here I met him.

Rest in peace Edward.

"THE LITTLE CHAP"

Across the void of time your voice echoes
Out from your life and on into another age,
Where I have listened silently to deeds of long ago
While my life moves apace, from page to page.

I heard you and in hearing, think I know you,
Then in autumnal fields of France I chance upon
Your resting place and it's my honour now to show you
My deep respect, bravest of England's sons

How still, this copse wherein you lie beneath the sod,
Sleep on, you are indeed, "A soldier known to God"
And I who heard you, now have met you, journey's end,
A friendship forged across the years, Edward my friend.

TERRY CARTER ON "VISITING"

I have been down into the cellar in Avril Williams' farmhouse accommodation at Auchonvillers many times over the last few years and, to be honest, when she gives her cellar tour and talk to her guests, I do not listen any more. I hope you do not find me rude for saying that, but I have heard Avril's description of the cellar and its uses so many times that I know its history like the back of my hand. I prefer to just stand in the background, away from the group, and let my imagination run wild. Avril has no electric light in the cellar, she lights a small candle that she puts on a ledge in a small alcove set into the end wall. The only other light is a 'glimmer' of daylight down the cellar steps from the entrance above.

I try to imagine what it would have been like to have experienced life in the cellar during 1916. The steps leading down into it would have been somewhere to sit down. It would have been impossible to go up into the original farmhouse as it would have been a pile of rubble. I can imagine the corner entrance, which was made so that the cellar was at trench level, with sacking material hanging from the doorway to act as a gas curtain. I also imagine the muffled barrage of distant artillery and the louder crashes as shells land ever nearer. The candle flickers and dust falls from the cracks in the ceiling. The hairs on the back of my neck stand up as I visualise a soldier turning to his mate and saying, "Bloody hell, that was close!", or another, silhouetted by candlelight, scratching his name onto the cellar wall with the tip of his bayonet. I see, in my mind's eye, the cellar full of exhausted stretcher bearers, dead on their feet, after struggling to bring in wounded from the front line; a fifteen minute walk nowadays, but in 1916 they would have had to carry a casualty back through a maze of communication trenches, a journey that could have taken hours. Consider also what the smell would have been like? Unwashed bodies, and other aromas, the musty smell of wet clothes, the smell of cordite and, of course, the smell of death.

What must it have been like for men going up to the front line? Staying one night in the ruins of Auchonvillers before relieving another battalion, manning the front line, the following night. How would a soldier have felt knowing that he would soon have to leave the safety of this cellar and make his way down, amid constant shellfire, thinking that in a few hours he would have to fix his bayonet and, on the blast of an officer's whistle, get out of the trench and advance to the German wire amid a stream of machine gun and small arms fire . . . and if he gets through that, will he be held up by rows of uncut barbed wire? Now that is something I cannot imagine, nor do I want to, but it is the kind of thing that Paul tries to visualise and capture in his poetry on our walks.

All is not, however, "doom and gloom" on these excursions and, in order to "take on fuel", our first stopping place on any visit to the Somme area is 'The Tommy Bar' at Poziers, to say "hello" to the owner, Dominic, and sample his "refreshment". On a recent visit, an acquaintance, who I had met on a previous visit to Auchonvillers, popped in. He told us that he was involved in an archaeological dig on farmland near Serre Road No.2 Cemetery on a project involving the war service of Wilfred Owen, the war poet, as part of a TV documentary. This was of interest to us all, in view of the involvement of the 8th and 6th Royal Warwicks in this area, and my research into them, so without further ado we made our way there.

On arrival, we were surprised and excited, to see that the dig was taking place in the region of the front line trench of the German Heidenkopf Redoubt. Luckily, I had all my research about the attack by the Warwicks in a folder with me, but knowing how fussy 'archaeological types' are, we stood on the edge of the road adjacent to the dig hoping someone would come over and have a chat. Luckily, someone did, it was the archaeologist in overall charge. He explained to us all about what was going on and why. I then told him about my interest and that, where they were digging, men from the 8th and 6th Royal Warwicks would have crossed over the trench and some would have probably occupied it at some stage on 1st July 1916. I then showed him my maps, etc., with which he was so impressed that he proceeded to give us a guided tour of the dig and showed us the trenches that had been excavated. It was a privilege to be taken round and shown this area, which had not seen the light of day in 85 years. The most poignant sights were three shallow indentations in the mud, each with a small wooden cross with a poppy attached. During the excavation, the remains of three bodies had been found, one British and two German.

These newly discovered remains will have been interred, albeit belatedly, with full military honours in a relevant war cemetery after identification, or failing this being possible, as "soldiers known unto God".

It was in just such a cemetery, Flatiron Copse Cemetery in Caterpillar Valley, that Paul was inspired to write about Corporal Edward Dwyer VC. The Somme abounds with these cemeteries, and I shall be referring to one of them later on in the book, but for now I would like to offer a word on the Battlefields themselves. As we have seen, they are still, essentially, war graves. The Heidenkopf has just released three of its sleepers some 85 years after they were taken. The fields, described so well by Paul in the poem "Sunbathing", therefore, deserve, and must have, respect. After the autumn harvest they still yield the iron harvest of war, extreme care must be taken. One of the main reasons that Paul and I have for visiting the battlefield is to retrace the steps of a certain battalion which may have connections with our home town or city. This invariably means a detour, "off the beaten track" having due regard for the privacy of local farmers' property.

We enjoy walking the fields and tracks, visiting little cemeteries that that seldom have visitors and, by going in spring or autumn, many fields are empty of crops and the white stain of chalk on the surface of the soil indicates former trench lines and zones of heavy shell-fire. I take copies of trench maps with me to trace the movements of the many battalions of the Royal Warwickshire Regiment that served on the Somme during 1916. We try and stick to the farm tracks but sometimes we have to walk over fields which are private property and permission should be asked for, and always is.

When walking on the Somme, it is impossible not to find a battlefield relic of some kind as Paul has described in his poem, The Bayonet. A jagged piece of rusty shell-shard, shrapnel balls, spent bullets, bits of phosphor bronze driving band from a shell casing or more personal items like a brass buckle from a soldiers webbing or a button from a tunic or shirt. However, amongst this detritus of war, that the soil produces year after year is live ammunition. Bullets, hand-grenades, Stokes Mortars and unexploded shells of all sizes and calibres. During the harvest, farm hands usually stockpile any live shells and hand grenades in a corner of a field. These are supposed to be collected by the French military to be disposed of. Perhaps, with really large calibre howitzer shells, this may be the case. But, in our years of visiting the Somme, we see many small groups of shells lying rusting …. still live, still there, and never moved.

A seasoned visitor to the battlefield should know that nothing that is live, or looks as if it might be live, should picked up. The reason I say this may bring a smile to the reader's face. A couple of years ago I visited the Somme with a friend who was making his first visit. He had no special interest in the Great War, but just wanted to join us to find out what we find so special in visiting the Somme.

Walking down a farm track, towards where we parked the car, we passed two or three unexploded shells lying in the undergrowth. Our "first time visitor" asked why they were put there. Jokingly, I told him that the farmer leaves them there and if anyone wants one as a souvenir, they can help themselves! I took it for granted he knew I was joking ……..

Once we got back to the car, we did what most men do when they are caught short out in a field in the middle of nowhere, we decided to take a leak behind some bushes. Meanwhile our "first time visitor", who had not realised that I was joking, had gone back, picked up the live shell and, holding it in both arms, came walking down the track. When asked what he was doing, he replied that he thought it would make a nice memento for his son! On being informed that the shell was probably live, and could be extremely dangerous, he gingerly deposited it at the side of the track, whilst watching the rest of the party running away down the track, hastily zipping up! Three more possible casualties of the Somme! But the sensible moral of the tale is, photograph any ordnance relics in situ, and leave them where they are!

3

MOVING UP THE LINE

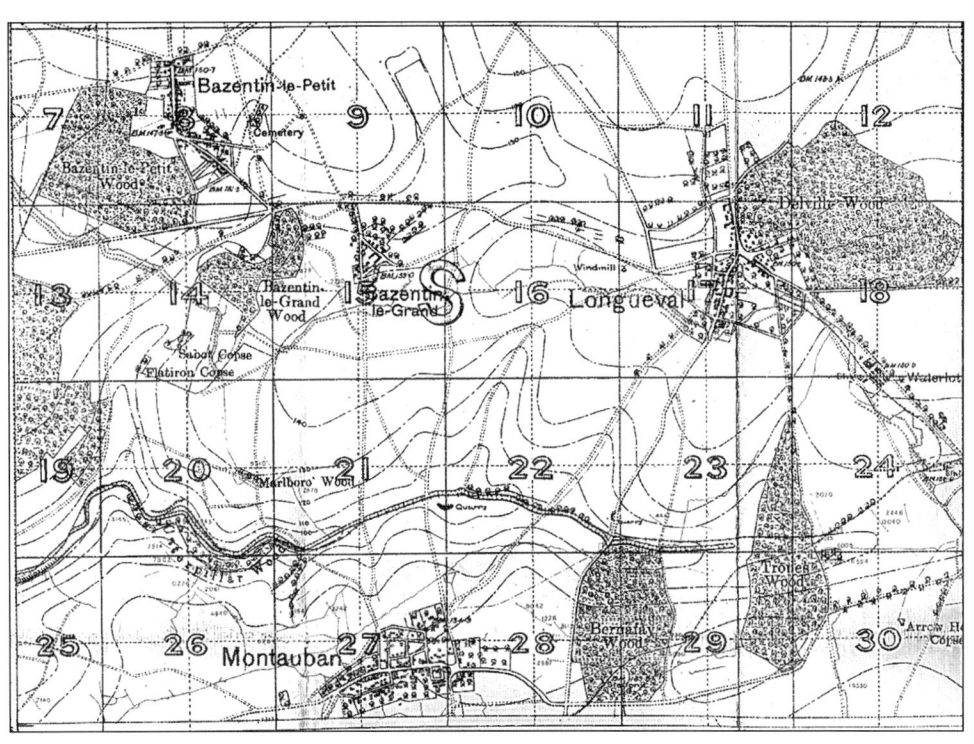

EXPERIENCE

I have watched most of the film footage relating to the Somme battlefields, shown in cinemas at home around 1916 and after, and have seen the rows of 'Tommies' advancing up to their positions at the front, cheering, smiling and waving their helmets.

Some of our walks from Auchonvillers have centred around Serre Road and the respective positions held by troops, who would later give everything in the July to November battle. These positions were a respectable distance behind the front line and, whilst walking between the two positions, I have often considered the thoughts of those moving up and perhaps more poignantly, those moving out of the line (if they could make the journey unaided). There must have been, in my opinion, mixed feelings. For those going up; anticipation, fear and excitement. For those coming back; relief, disbelief and regret at what they had seen and been part of. It would only be natural for new and inexperienced troops to try to "pick the brains" of those who had been there, but to what avail? Those who had experienced the horrors of war would not, in my view, want to relive them for the entertainment or education of others. What of those maimed, wounded, blinded or mentally scarred? They would each be carrying their own individual crosses which would probably burden them for the rest of their lives Those who were so terribly injured, would not have had any quality to the rest of their lives. This poem is by way of an apology to them; the search for someone else's experiences often results in additional pain for the sufferer. We were all once young, inquisitive and only learned by our own and others' experiences, it's called life!

EXPERIENCE

As we moved up, we met him sitting in the sun,
Unseeing eyes his gift to England and it made no sense,
For we were young and we were soldiers, virgin guns,
We asked him as we passed, of his experience,
And so he gave us what we asked for, told us tales,
And filled with deepest dread each empty head,
And each blank canvas daubed with colours pale,
"I cannot truly tell you what it's like", he said,
"But you will tell your own tales soon" and turned
His head away, we could not see his sightless eyes,
We stood and watched, each one of us his lesson learned.
"How old are you?", we asked as he, helplessly, tried to rise,
He turned unseeing eyes to us and he replied
"Eighteen next January, but today I died".

THE LAST TIME

The journey to the Somme battlefields starts with a ferry crossing and it was whilst watching the receding cliffs of Dover on my last trip that that this poem came to mind. At the time of The Great War there was, obviously, no Channel Tunnel, so every soldier from England would have followed this route at some stage. My thoughts then went to the many railway stations and to the silent film footage, often seen, of soldiers waving cheerily from railway carriage windows. How unpredictable life is and what a tenuous grip we have on it. People were saying goodbye and in the case of many, it was the last time they would do so. The next communication would be the dreaded telegram and all the hopes that they had would, in that instant, disappear.

The word "goodbye" is a strange word, shortened from "God be with you". When a mother, sister or fiancée said these words to her departing soldier, what did she mean, and what did he mean? How long was God to be with them? For life, in death, who knows? One thing is, however, certain and that is, that death is inevitable, it is only the timing which is unknown. The tragedy is, that this "Great" war greatly shortened the life expectancy of millions who marched on "unwary feet".

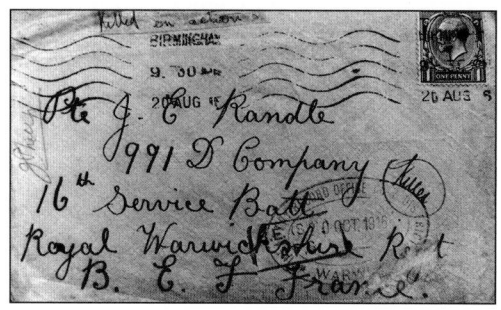

THE LAST TIME

How silently the last time
Creeps in and we do not know
That this is indeed the last chime
Of the clock and it's time to go;
Carried on winds which take me away
From the things which matter the most
And the dreams, which I had, fall into decay
And my thoughts become so many ghosts.

The last time that we embraced,
We were simply saying goodbye,
Unaware of the horrors so soon to be faced,
Not knowing that soon I would die;
So learn that goodbye is a warning,
Remember till next time we meet
That death listens out every morning,
For the footfalls of unwary feet.

TERRY CARTER ON "MOVING UP THE LINE"

When I read the poems in this section, I immediately thought of the many letters written by two sweethearts from Birmingham in the Great War, Private Jim Randle of D Company, 3rd Birmingham Battalion (16th Royal Warwicks) and his girl, Ethel Wray. Most are written by Jim, and tell of his training and his first (and last) months of overseas service.

In a letter written in June 1916 whilst at Arras, Jim, probably as a result of not having written for a few days, writes, *"Just to let you know I am amongst the land of the living"*. He continues with, *"I am still merry and bright. There are still one or two of us who keep smiling and no-one will knock that smile off, if we can help it, and we are bursting to have a good scrap, just to see what it is like"*. What Jim refers to here is, that since arriving in France on 21st November 1915, the battalion had only been in trench holding duties, most of the time repairing those that been damaged by shell fire or bad weather. So far they had not seen any offensive action. However, with the benefit of hindsight, we know that the 'Battle of the Somme' is just around the corner.

On 12th June 1916, his company were in reserve trenches midway between Arras and the Roclincourt and Jim had enough time to put pen to paper for another letter to Ethel. In this letter he tells Ethel about the good luck that has befallen himself and his friend who Jim refers to as 'Windows' (I presume because he wore glasses). *"We only get together now when we get out of the trenches owing to one (of us) being a bomber and the other being a company runner. I think I have finished going in the firing line now, I am company runner, it's not so dangerous"*.

Oh Jim! If I could only go back in time and tell you that in the forthcoming action, being a company runner was one of the most dangerous duties. This letter finishes with, *"Well dear, I am sending you my watch as a souvenir because I shall only lose it or get it smashed knocking about the trenches"*. Perhaps Jim made the comment about the company runner being not so dangerous to give Ethel peace of mind. Perhaps he guessed at the dangers which lay ahead and that's why he sent his watch to her.

For the first two weeks of July 1916, Jim's division were part of GHQ Reserve and still in the Arras region. Then orders came through for them to march south and join the Battle of the Somme.

Jim wrote one more letter which Ethel received on 8th July, and on 25th July he managed to send a Field Post Card, *"I am quite well and hope to be discharged soon, I have received your letter dated 25th July 1916, letter follows at first opportunity"*.

Two days later Jim was dead. There were no remains to bury, he must have been blown off the face of the earth. After the successful British advance on 14th July along the Bazentin Ridge, German troops had stubbornly held onto the northern ruins of Longueval, Delville Wood and High Wood. On 27th July, two brigades were ordered to attack the northern portion of Longueval and the western edge of Delville Wood (15 Bde 5th div and 99 BDE 2nd div). As both brigades got into position and prepared for the assault, the German artillery kept up a heavy barrage on the southern approaches to Longueval. In return, the British artillery were firing on the northern approaches of the pulverised remains of the village. Consequently, the attack, which was to involve Jim's division, was to take place within a curtain of incessant shell fire. News getting back to the battalion and brigade headquarters regarding progress of the attack, depended on any survivors getting through this ring of destruction. How was news supposed to get back? Yes, you guessed it . . company runner.

The Platoon Commander of Jim's D company was 19 year old Second Lieutenant Thomas Pearman, who, many years later, wrote a brief memoir concerning his experience during the horrendous shell fire, the desolation and mounds of dead:

"I remember taking what was left of my platoon back to the edge of the wood. There we linked up with another Subaltern named Rowlands (also D company) who had survived untouched. He told me he was quite certain he was going to be killed and I tried to cheer him up. Shortly afterwards I had the urge to check upon my platoon further on. When I came back to meet Rowlands he was not there nor the men who had been there with him. A giant shell had taken the lot or buried them. I can remember scratching in the earth, calling Rowlands and then losing consciousness."

Second Lieutenant Rowlands, Private Jim Randle and the majority of men killed on this date are now commemorated on the Thiepval Memorial. Private Jim Randle's name appeared in the Official Casualty List on 6th September 1916.

Back in Birmingham, Ethel was getting quite concerned she had not heard from Jim for a few weeks. So, on 19th August, she wrote the following letter, not knowing that Jim had been dead for three weeks.
"Dear Jim,

I am writing again to you, hoping you are quite well and safe. No doubt you are very busy but if you could drop me field card if you cannot write a letter, as I have not heard from you since 8th July. Really we are all very anxious about you. I sent you a parcel on the 23rd July. I have not heard if you have received it yet. I do hope there is nothing seriously the matter. I wrote to you from Much Wenlock but I thought I would wait a few days thinking you might answer it. Fred is also very anxious about you. I think he is writing to you. Hoping to hear some good news from you soon. So with kind regards from all at home, and my best love to yourself, I remain yours Ethel XXXX."

The letter was returned to Ethel from the Royal Warwickshire Record Office. Scribbled on the envelope above Jim's name was, "Killed in Action".

On 22nd August 1916, Jim's pal, Private W G Moss No.921 wrote to Ethel:

"Dear Miss,

I am writing this letter to inform you of the death of my friend Private Jim Randle who was killed in action on 27th July. As one of Jimmy's chums I must express to you the deep regret which is felt by the fellows left in the platoon. Jim was always the best of pals and I feel his loss very keenly, knowing you were a very close friend of his I must sympathise with you in your bereavement. Please let me know that you have received this letter and oblige.

Yours respectfully, W G Moss."

This is one sad set of letters relating to one young girl losing a loved one. Multiply it a few thousand times and the scale of the tragedy of the Somme becomes clearer.

4

AT THE FRONT

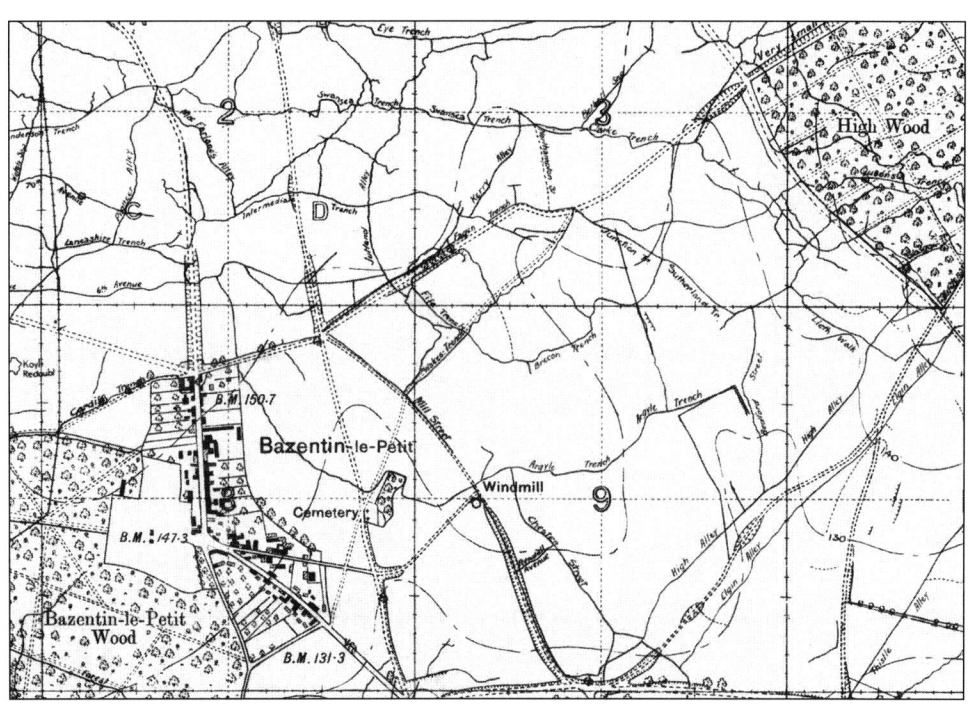

DOUBT

A man who has had great influence on my poetry and who was, in my view, a hero, is Siegfried Sassoon. His poetry is extremely well written, powerful and reflects his growing disillusionment with the prolonging of the war, for what he saw as political, as opposed to military ends. He was a decorated officer who led his men with great bravery and toward the end of the war was wrongly labelled, by some, as a conscientious objector. His life story is fascinating and well worth studying.

This poem, which came into my head whilst studying the battle-scarred crucifix at Crucifix Corner, is an attempt to portray the thoughts, which must have gone through many heads in their suffering, that the sights which they had seen and the experiences they had been through were enough to shake even the most vehement faith. If any army loses faith in its leaders and the leaders are not properly led themselves, those at the bottom of the pile come out worst. Many lads had joined up with enthusiasm, to "do their bit". This increasingly came to mean remaining static for long periods and then putting oneself up as a slowly moving target silhouetted against the sky line of Picardy, for the enemy to "pick off" almost at will. Is it any wonder then, that even the strongest faith was tested?

DOUBT

I thought that life was worth far more than this
And I believed that only my own God was good,
They said this show was far too good to miss,
I never questioned them, but now I think I should.

They used brave words to me and I was not afraid,
I clung to them steadfastly and the things I knew,
To them and my true god, daily, I prayed,
But now I wonder if those words were true.

FUTILITY

I do not know how I would have reacted if I had been called upon to face the horrors that our army faced throughout the war and, in particular, the months of July to November 1916 on the Somme.

It seems to me, from the many books which I have read about a soldier's life at the front, that for the most part life was one of hard physical labour, punctuated by periods of high activity and mounting terror.

Who knows what the lads were thinking before facing up to their fears and advancing over the top? Initially, there may have been belief in the words of their commanders that they would walk to and through, the enemy lines, but surely, for the survivors, the evidence of their own eyes would have given lie to that suggestion in a very short time. So, from then on, I suspect they would have believed that there was a very good chance of meeting their end at any time. Whatever their hopes, dreams and aspirations, they would have had to accept that these, along with themselves, may soon be snuffed out. How do you measure bravery such as this?

FUTILITY

Before I die I have to find the time
To end this short life's chorus with a rhyme,
For soon I shall be face to face with death,
Crying for life but knowing, in my mind, I'm wasting breath.
There is no reason why I die, I'm loathe to leave
This life, but in my heart I know there's no reprieve
And so bravely I'll rise, young jaw firm set,
Passing unmarked, the chalk the only grave I'll get,
Rising this summer morning under cloudless sky,
Within the hour, my demons and my dreams will die.

WAITING

I think that the life of a soldier "at the front" must have been one of long periods of physical labour and short periods of mayhem, all spent under the constant fear of the relentless shell fire and the overriding thought that, tomorrow may be their last day alive.

It is difficult to imagine what those endless days and nights of monotony may have been like from our viewpoint of ninety years in the future but, at least, an idea can be gleaned by visiting the wonderful Trench Museum at the rear of the "Tommy Bar" at Poziers. Here the owner Dominic has recreated a trench system complete with dugouts, using original artefacts by the thousand. Each year it gets better and, on my last visit, we were given a night time tour, lit only by candles, which was both spectacular and eerie. Full marks to Dominic for creating this living museum but, whilst it is of great interest to visit, I reiterate that such a visit can only give a tiny insight into what actual conditions must have been like. In addition, whilst it may be possible to recreate locations, I believe it is impossible to recreate two important aspects; noise and fear. Life must have been very much a lottery. A chance shell could wipe it out and no matter how many prayers were offered up, if it was your turn, that was it. The idea for this poem came about on my last visit to the Tommy Bar. I have done the best I can but I believe it may only scratch the surface of the feelings of those who suffered deprivation and boredom under death's constant threat.

WAITING

The endless days slip silent into night,
The candle marks the hours as they slip by
Seemingly endless, sun and stars fade out of sight
And men learn how to kill and how to die.
Each day in passing, totters on the brink and falls
Into that pit those who survive will call the past,
While those who die enter ancestral halls,
What difference will it mean to either at the last?
We tire of waiting, dull of wit, desolate of mind,
In stagnant pools, by bloody stalemate confined
And time passes us by, as if we were not there,
Cocooned within this nether world where we invoke
Protection from our Gods, to them we swear
Allegiance, yet our lives may still go up in smoke.

ALL OUT

I have yet to walk the battlefields in the dark. Some of my friends have done this and regaled me with their tales, but, as yet, I have not, and don't know if I ever will. I believe that, susceptible as I am to imagination which in turn breeds inspiration, the experience might be hard for me to come to terms with.

Of course it has to be borne in mind that much of the activity in these fields took place in daylight hours. Night was, usually, a time for rest, raids and watching. Sentry duty must have been dreadful, the darkness of night, the occasional flare, the odd round discharged and the raiding parties. How many went out, how many returned? On their forays they may have encountered those previously wounded or worse. What horror that must have been! "All Out" was inspired on an evening walk around Auchonvillers when I got to thinking about sentries. It was a court martial offence to sleep on such duty, yet, dog tired, they had to scan the black void for raiders, or returning night patrols, listening for the whispered password to allow them in. What became of those who were discovered in their raiding activity? A quick burst and no more, pale ghosts blasted into the night yet still, the sentry must keep vigilant, knowing that the dawn would bring the next barrage and the renewed carnage which accompanied it. What bravery!

ALL OUT

Shrouded in darkness, yet alert, erect,
Night's cloak enfolding, yet he must not sleep,
Crouched in the clay, as the night winds creep
Around him, while the silent stars reflect
Hardness of heart, reflected in numbness of brain,
Wind in the wire sounds out its requiem
For those before, "Requiescant in Pacem"
This silent night their everlasting dead domain.
No sound breaks, save that the angry dead cry out,
As the pale moon emerges from a cloud's dark rim
And disappears: still vigilant, he casts his eyes about,
No dark returning shapes to challenge him,
Those who went out, he searches for, as in a trance,
But night has blasted them to insignificance.

A FINAL THOUGHT

The opening stanza of this poem was inspired by one written by Rupert Brooke, on a different theme, at the beginning of the war. His poem reflects the excitement and adventure of the coming conflict. He did not, unfortunately, live to participate much in the 'excitement' as he died of disease in its early stages. Thus, he was spared the disillusionment experienced and portrayed by that other Great War poet Siegfried Sassoon.

This poem just came into my head one day. I can't remember where I was walking exactly and it doesn't matter. The fields of the Somme are a rich and constant source of inspiration to me.

You may think that this poem is slightly flippant, I may agree, but I am trying to portray the acceptance by those who fought on these fields that death, or at least injury, was, to some extent, inevitable. It was just a matter of 'when' not 'if' and the real regret I have is that this fate was suffered, in the main, by those who didn't truly understand why things were as they were. They had joined up to fight and fight they did, but I am sure that their idea of what awaited them did not correspond to that which they ultimately endured. The Great War was a war of machinery, machinery of killing. The old ideals and values had gone, last seen in Flanders at Christmas in 1914 in the temporary truce. That collaboration had been frowned upon and stopped, now it was every man for himself and if your number was up, that's how it was.

Faced with this inescapable truth, I admire the philosophical attitude of our troops, who endured and suffered with honour and acceptance. The bluntness with which I have written this poem is meant to reflect this attitude. You may call it flippancy if you will.

A FINAL THOUGHT

Now thank we all our God, that one's gone wide,
Which doesn't help my mates on my left side,
Each time the planned trajectory falls short
Gives me this fleeting moment, 'til the next retort
Announces to me, crushed beneath this weight of fear,
The single, simple, truth, that life is dear
And in particular, this one, soon to be snuffed out
Without an answer to my question, "What was it all about?".

PRAYER

The cemeteries on the Somme are places of great beauty and calm. I have seen many at first hand and watched footage of those who were lost being interred in them. Of course, the films did not benefit from sound and I, therefore, have no idea of what the internment service consisted of, but I expect it was fairly short due to prevailing circumstances.

I have also seen footage of 'church parades' and drumhead services prior to battle and again, I have no idea of what such a service might have consisted of, but, whilst walking the tracks around the edge of High Wood, the accompanying poem started to form in my mind. I have tried to keep it simple and I would venture to hope that, by the time that the battles of the Somme and Ancre were fought, the wisdom of the war was being questioned by those who fought it.

What is to be admired, however, is that they carried on. Whether they knew where the blame for their predicament lay is open to question, but I should like to think that those who were charged with their spiritual guidance may have had a thought for those whose decisions were sending their charges into imminent danger of death. I believe that this "Great" war was thought to be the "war to end wars" and that, as such, once finished, lasting peace would ensue. I wanted this soldier's prayer to echo this thought. I don't know if I have succeeded. You must judge.

PRAYER

Lord

I, who have walked life's path with thee
And loved each day of joy and laughter,
Know, here might be the end of me,
So grant this wish; that ever after
I am gone, this war will not
Condemn those, whose lives are linking
Hearts and minds with shell and shot,
Spare them, oh Lord, let not my sinking
Into death be all in vain,
No! Let my passing cure their fever,
Calming the storms of warlike brains
And let that calm endure forever.

Amen

TERRY CARTER ON "AT THE FRONT"

This section of Paul's book contains poems which reflect, I think, on the everyday existence of lads in the front line. Every day was spent in carrying out necessary tasks to ensure the integrity of the line against a background of the chance of imminent death or disfigurement. Paul's poems seem to me to delve into the mind of the front line soldier, his doubts, his fears and his prayers, The one which really springs out to me, however, is "All Out" summing up very well the dark hours and the inevitable sentry duty, night patrols, and raids over the strip of land known as No Man's Land. The opposing lines meandered over the landscape and, therefore, the width of No Man's Land varied from being a stone's throw apart to a couple of hundred yards or more. The Germans dug deep trenches lined with wooden planks and wooden staircases leading down to deep galleries of dugouts which could hold vast quantities of men and material. The vast industrial region of northern France and its coalfields were under German occupation, so the German munitions industry had the raw power to keep in full production. They were quite happy to stay put in their trenches and run the war on their terms.

The British, however, had a different point of view. Our trenches were only dug on a temporary basis, they were not considered to be permanent defensive positions like the German lines. Our trenches were there solely to provide a "jumping off" line for the next offensive and No Man's Land, right up to the German barbed wire, was considered our land. Patrols were a means of gathering information to find out which troops held the opposing trenches and of familiarising the troops with ground they would need to cross in any future attack. Patrols in No Man's Land also offered a good "proving experience" for young subalterns fresh from the U.K.

By 1916 the majority of newly commissioned Second Lieutenants were fresh out of school or college. The terror of leaving the trench and cautiously inching their way forward, on their stomachs, across shell torn terrain towards the German wire with flares going off overhead and machine guns traversing in front would "make a man out of them", in the estimation of their generals.

If a flare went up, men would freeze in place. Their natural instinct was to duck, dodge, or drop prone, but the slightest movement would draw fire, usually from expert snipers. Sometimes the enemy would simply fire at noise, or merely into the darkness hoping to hit someone. The Germans, also, sent out patrols for intelligence purposes and both sides would attempt to ambush each other if contact was made.

A few years ago I met a veteran of the 16th Royal Warwicks (3rd Birmingham Bn.) by the name of Ted Francis. He told me that he had always volunteered for the nightly patrols into No Man's Land. The reason being "that it got him out of the mundane routine of daily trench fatigues such as working parties or cleaning up the trenches". In addition, as a result of his nightly excursions, he was allowed to rest all the next day in his dugout.

Notices were frequently sent round to battalion commanders from Brigade Headquarters and beyond asking the question, "Are you being offensive enough?" To ensure that patrols went out and went close to the German lines, some senior officers had innocuous, but readily identifiable, items placed by previous patrols close to the enemy line with instructions that they should be brought back, by subsequent patrols, in order to prove that they had been "offensive enough". In addition to this kind of "initiative", I am sure Brigadier Generals or Divisional Commanders gained additional kudos from their superiors relative to the number of nightly patrols ordered out from their sector.

'Trench Raids' on the other hand, were usually terrifying affairs for both sides, involving hand-to-hand fighting in cramped spaces and in pitch dark. Sometimes they involved only a handful of men, on others a few hundred. All had one intention, to cut through the German wire, enter a section of front line trench and cause as much chaos as possible in the shortest space of time before the Germans could bring up reinforcements and retaliate. Mills grenades, bayonets, knives and a vast array of home made cudgels and coshes bristling with spikes and bolts were the usual weapons of trench-fighting. To prevent the Germans gaining any intelligence, in the event of death or capture of any of the raiders, all personal identification was left behind and shoulder titles were always removed from tunics. Brass buttons were blackened and burnt cork or black grease-paint smeared onto faces with balaclavas being worn instead of steel helmets. On some raids our artillery put down what was known as a 'box barrage' on the section of German trench to be raided. This helped prevent any counter-attack attempting to repel the raiders. On other occasions 'blocks' were put in at either end of a section of German trench. The 'block' consisted of a couple of men with bayonets and a couple more with Mills Bombs which prevented Germans counter-attacking around the traverse of a trench. Meanwhile, the raiders would wreak as much havoc as they could, killing and throwing bombs down into the deep dugouts. Apart from gaining information from any prisoners that were captured, these raids kept the German troops in all sections of the front line on tenterhooks wondering if their section were to be next for a raid.

Those who took part in patrols or trench raids considered that returning to their own trenches was the most dangerous part of the operation. Nervous sentries often fired at any movement in front of them and inadvertently caused many casualties by doing so. On one occasion a sentry killed two of his own men with one shot. It was not uncommon for men, on returning from a patrol or a raid, to be skewered by a British bayonet after jumping down into their own trenches.

5

INTO ACTION

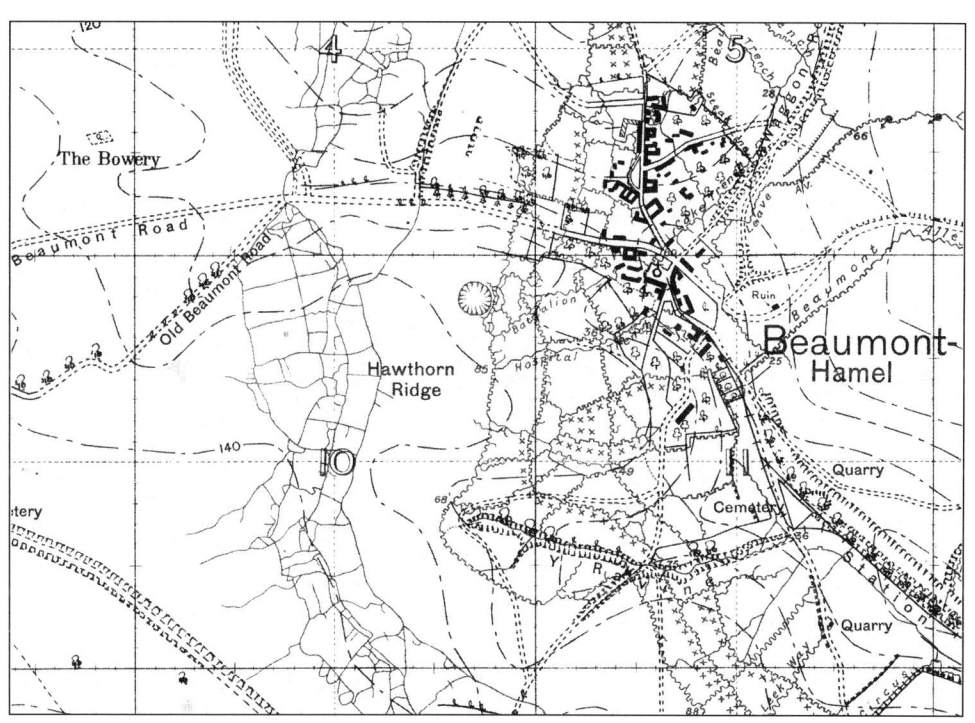

SHRAPNEL

The area to the south of High Wood is a place we always make for, because it has connections with the City Battalions of the Royal Warwickshire Regiment, which coming from Birmingham, are of special interest to Terry. The Germans held a corner of the wood and steadfastly resisted attempts to capture it. Even when gains were made they were not capitalised on and the initiatives were lost. The fields approaching High Wood from the direction of Longueval were killing grounds. Enemy machine gunners literally could not miss and many brave men died.

Walking, as we do, in these fields after the Autumn ploughing, the detritus of the war is still emerging and I was struck by the proliferation of shrapnel balls which I found on one such walk in this area. What a horrible weapon the shrapnel shell is, its prime purpose was to cut through barbed wire but, with adjustment, its preset fuse could be set to explode the shell at just above head height and thereby eject its load of over two hundred small lead balls in all directions to maim and kill. It is always rewarding to find remnants of war in the field but, in handling these particular objects, I am left to ponder what damage and injury these small lead balls inflicted in their fall to earth. These thoughts inspired this poem.

SHRAPNEL

Rainfall of iron fell on my world and split
That world apart, shard shower's fingers tore away
That which I once held dear, digging its pit
Deep in this tortured mind, still deeper into clay.

No field dressing can cover up this blistered land,
Nor perfume neutralise the stench, nor fragrant balm
Eradicate this fearfulness, nor still these trembling hands,
Nor take the terror from this mind and leave it calm.

I must endure as man, for such is my disguise,
While in my fear, I crawl about trying to climb
Back to myself, leaving my horrors where they lie
Deep rooted in this charnel house of time,
Where sightless eyes look to their god in empty rage
And I am left in witness to a Godless age.

AN UNGUARDED MOMENT

Newfoundland Park is well known to all visitors to the Somme area. Its visitor centre is impressive and informative. Here, we have a location where reserve troops, silhouetted against the skyline, were decimated by enemy fire before they had even reached their own front line.

This poem, which is one of several 'first person' poems in this book, was inspired by this place. Here, you can easily judge the normal distance between the two front lines, in this case, about 800 metres I think. I have tried here to put myself in the position of one of the unfortunate souls who did not survive the morning of 1st July 1916.

The anticipated attack was now a reality! The "walk to the enemy lines" was going to happen at last! Of course, there would be nervousness, fear even, but this was what the lads had joined up for, the adventure and excitement, to have a go at the Hun! In the last moments before attack, I think it would be only natural to be thinking of home and loved ones, but, there was a job to do. All was ready, the waiting was over. It may be, that once the inevitable happened and the whistle sounded, adrenalin would take over and fear might, for a short time, be replaced with confidence. What then would be the reaction of those brave lads, as they watched their pals dropping by their side, knowing that in all probability they would be next? I cannot begin to think. This poem is my humble attempt to portray their feelings and with my greatest respect, pays tribute to the sacrifice that took place here.

AN UNGUARDED MOMENT

Our time has come: fearful, yet resolute, we stand,
Ready at last, steel hard to the touch, cool to the hand,
Waiting is over, now is the hour, now as the sky
Turns hostile and all around death's probing fingers pry
Into the ether, on toward the enemy unseen,
We know now, that tedious weeks have merely been
Prelude to this, for now our time is here,
The time when dearer thoughts must help suppress our fear,
For this we waited and if morning air should fill
Minds with fond remembrance of another place, we will
All memory of other times and places, now forsake,
Put thoughts of future to one side for battle's sake.
The time of steel is here, the whistle's blast
Hangs in the summer air, we rise at last,
All is now chanced, yet as the minutes pass
Fear disappears as, leisurely, we wander through the grass,
And we grow confident, we long for cigarettes, our minds return
To windows where familiar faces shine and lights still burn,
In that unguarded moment, when strength is beyond doubt,
Then, all our memories and thoughts and lights go out.

TERRY CARTER ON "INTO ACTION"

To complement Paul's two very powerful poems in this section, I feel I can do no better than to quote directly from the diary of an NCO who served in the 14th Battalion, The Royal Warwickshire Regiment (1st Birmingham Battalion). The 14th along with the 15th Royal Warwicks (1st & 2nd Birmingham) served in the 13th Infantry Brigade of the 5th Division). The 5th Division was part of the original B.E.F. that went to France in August 1914 and had been involved in the thick of the fighting ever since. The three Birmingham Pals battalions plus the 12th Gloucesters did not transfer into the Division until January 1916. Birmingham's three 'Pals' battalions were raised during September 1914 from white collar workers within the city and outlying districts. Since arriving in France on 21st November 1914 they had only undertaken basic trench holding duties with occasional patrols into No Man's Land. The attack on the German held trench at Wood Lane, near High Wood, was to be the first 'Over the Top' action that the 1st and 2nd Birmingham Battalion's would be involved in. However, it was only a preliminary attack, the purpose of which was to advance and consolidate Wood Lane at 10pm on 22nd July 1916. At 1am on 23rd July the main attack would then take place to 'leap-frog' Wood Lane towards the German main front line known as the 'Switch Line.'

Eight days earlier, this ground had been a quiet area behind the German lines. Then on 14th July, 1916 a successful dawn attack had taken place, during which a foothold had been gained in the south-eastern corner of High Wood and a hastily dug slit trench had been dug along the bank of the road from High Wood to Longueval. This line had been first started by the men of the Secunderabad Cavalry Brigade, namely the 7th Dragoon Guards and the Indian 20th Deccan Horse after their cavalry charge, on the evening of 14th July, to cover the right flank of the infantry advancing on High Wood. The cavalry were relieved the next day and soon afterwards it was decided to retire back towards Bazentin le Petit whilst our artillery pounded High Wood and its adjacent area, hoping to destroy the cover the wood gave to its defenders. During this period the Germans began to construct a forward trench line down what is known as Wood Lane which, in one section, is deeply sunken and very hard to see and which would prove to be a very tough obstacle for British troops to attack over the ensuing weeks.

The second attempt to take High Wood and the Switch Line took place on 20th July. Troops of the 33rd Division advancing on High Wood and those of the 7th Division towards the Switch Line. Again, the Germans offered stubborn resistance and only the south-east corner of the wood could be occupied. It fell to the 2nd Gordon Highlanders and the 8th Devons (20th Brigade, 7th Division) to advance on Wood Lane. That too failed and both battalions retired back to the Martinpuich/Longueval Road where the cavalry had previously dug in. After darkness fell the 20th Brigade was replaced by 1st Royal West Kents and the 14th Royal Warwicks (1st Birmingham Bn.) of the 5th Division's 13th Brigade.

For two days the West Kents and Warwicks deepened their trench line, as the German artillery had calculated their range perfectly. The German line in Wood Lane was, in parts, a sunken road. Crops reached chest high in the remaining ground between the opposing lines. Our Forward Observation Officers had difficulty in seeing Wood Lane and could not range our guns onto it. Thus, it came about, that none of our shells were doing any damage at all. At the corner where Wood Lane meets High Wood the Germans had constructed a formidable strongpoint bristling with machine-guns. Likewise, at the other end of Wood Lane another strongpoint had been created. Any advance across this strip of cornfield would be criss-crossed by decimating machine gun fire. Proposals for the next attack, on the evening the evening of 22nd July, were issued. At 10pm the 1st West Kents and 14th Royal Warwicks were to advance, take Wood Lane and consolidate. It would be then used as the "jumping off" trench for the second part of the attack towards the Switch Line at 1am on 23rd July. As the reader may guess, the attack proved to be a complete failure. The 14th Royal Warwicks suffered 485 casualties of which 205 were killed. The majority of these men were never found and their names are now commemorated on Thiepval Memorial. Here follows an extract from the diary of one of the wounded survivors of that terrible failed attack.

Diary extract of Corporal Arthur K Cooper, No.65, A Company, 1st Birmingham Battalion (14th Royal Warwicks).

Attack on Wood Lane, near High Wood, that took place on the night of 22nd/23rd July, 1916.

"7am on board the hospital boat Panama now, waiting to sail for Blighty, I came on board last night but we did not sail because some Hun Subs are outside. They sank five boats yesterday and I believe this port is closed till they catch them. We are kicking up our heels here waiting and impatient to get home, so I thought that it would help to keep my blood cool and keep my temperature down and therefore save unnecessary medicine, to continue to write a few notes. I don't know that I can remember a great lot about what's happened lately, the last fortnight or so, but I will do my best...........

I think the date was 22nd July. At ten o 'clock pm we got over the top and filed away into the gloom. I had my section in file behind me, which was the way we were to go forward until we were fairly close. This offers a small target for artillery fire, but of course as soon as the rifle fire gets hot we have to extend into line. I think that they must have had scouts well out in front of their line as, fairly early, their guns opened out like Hell and so did the rifle and machine-gunfire. They must have had hundreds of the latter. We extended and went forward at the double. The boys were dropping fairly thickly then and the line was very thin. I got to within about twenty yards of their trench where I could see the line of machine guns and rifles spitting fire, when I felt a sudden twinge through my right arm, which knocked my rifle out of my hand. I stooped to pick it up and at the same time I got a bash on the head with shrapnel and saw some real stars floating about. Then I knew no more for I can't say what period, but I came round some time later not feeling very well. Fritz was peppering away, so I knew that the boys had not moved him on this journey and that made me sad.

Anyway, I soon found out that the spot where I lay was not a very healthy one. I stood a good chance of stopping one from both ways, so I decided to move as soon as I possibly could, also taking into consideration Fritz's bits of lead which I was praying would cease before light set in. They did not, the swines kept on, so I decided to take my chance and crawl if I could. I tried two or three times before I got away and then only got a few yards before I dropped exhausted. Eventually and by small degrees I got about twenty yards and dropped into a bit of a shell hole. I dropped on the top of some other fellow. I don't know who he was, but he yelled out and some time after disappeared. He tried to get me to go on, but I absolutely could not and kept dropping off unconscious. Some time during the night I heard a voice asking me who I was. It was Tommy Thompson out of No. 3 platoon. He was hit in the thigh" (Private Victor Herbert Thompson, No.311, of Beaufort Road, Edgbaston).

(By the way, we have just started for Blighty 9am, August 12th)

'*Tommy and I could not give one another much help, I had lost a lot of blood through my head and arm by this time."*

(The bally boat has stopped. I wonder what the matter is. I wish this boat would go on. We have been stuck here in the open sea for half an hour. Must be a Sub, I think).

"*Well Tommy began to worry me to get a move on with him, but we both wanted help and neither one of us could help the other. I asked him to try and get in himself and I would come as soon as I could, but he couldn't shift. I thought that there was a good chance of us finishing our young careers there, as we were not likely to improve stopping out with our wounds not dressed. Oh! I forgot to say that I had a field dressing put very roughly on my head. I don't know if it was in the right place. I don't think it was. The fellow whom I dropped on when I first got into the shell hole put it on for me. Of course he couldn't see in the dark and I was not very sure where it was at the time.*

'*There was blood all over my head. Well I dropped off again and when I came to, morning had broken. That meant staying there until dark at any rate, because we were in view of Fritz and he would have soon finished us off if we had crept out. I* thought to myself, what a cheerful and bright day we were going to have! I had dropped my equipment in the first place. I couldn't carry it and I hadn't even got a drop of water. The happy day wore on.

Each side was shelling heavily and we were in the middle. Well, not quite, as we were only about forty yards from Fritz and I think that most of the shells which were shaking us were our own. Not very cheering lying down there thinking every minute that one of your own shells was going to wipe you out! Later in the day Tommy got hit again with shrapnel and so did I. This time in the left arm, not at all seriously though, mine was very slight, but I am afraid that my friend's was worse. So we went on through the day and when night fell we were both worse than we had been the previous night, but I made up my mind that we had got to get in and tried to kid Tommy to get a move on, but I couldn't shift him. In the end I started off on my own, crawling a very few yards at a time and how I eventually got there I have no idea. I remember the sentry challenging me and I could just say who I was. I then tried to get a couple of the fellows to come with me for Tommy, but they would not let me go, so I explained where he was and they said they would fetch him, I don't know if they ever found him. (Unfortunately, Private Victor Herbert Thompson was never found. He is named on the Thiepval Memorial.)

Two fellows, I think they were wounded, helped me down to the trench dressing station and I only remember being carried on the stretcher, a motor ambulance, more dressing stations, one where they gave me some beef-tea, which I gulped down red hot. I hadn't had anything, not even a drink, for about thirty hours. Then another motor ride to the rear and then the hospital, I woke up when the orderly was getting my clothes off. I had my wounds dressed and was washed all over and put into clean sheets. Ye Gods! What rest! Like dropping into heaven, but Oh my head! Someone was surely hitting it with a stick! It did give me Jib! I also found that I could not open one eye and I could only see very little out of the other and only stand having it open for a very short time. I was rather afraid that my right eye was done in through the wound in my head.

'I had about four or five days absolute agony and then underwent an operation to my head. I was sort of semi-conscious all the time during the operation. They seemed to be cracking all the bones in my head. It was just about the worst hour I have ever spent in my life. After that I gradually improved and on about the twelfth day my head was not singing and I got my first night's sleep in hospital. Previously my head at night got worse and worse until morning, when I was absolutely worn out. I didn't tell you I found a pal in Hospital. Private Newman, the son of the Tobacco people (No.319, W H Newman of Margaret Grove, Edgbaston), he was out of No.2 platoon. We got our beds put side by side and now we were getting better it was a great comfort to have a pal. On about the 6th I opened my right eye and by doing so just missed another operation which the doctor intended carrying out that day. I was very lucky.

My sight was improving fast now and I could read a bit, which made things a lot better for me. I began to take interest in my food, which is always a good sign and also had two servings of pudding. The sisters here are absolute angels and the doctor is a very nice man and also a very clever one. He told me on the 9th that he was sending me home, and on the 11th, I got carried on board and here I am still, 4pm, 12th, stuck still just outside the Harbour.

We stayed outside the harbour until about 6pm, and then off we went. I went to sleep and woke up at Southampton. I had my ticket marked No.3 District, which is Birmingham and the Midlands, but, although there was a Midland Railway train in for Birmingham and the North, to my great disappointment I was not put on it. Instead I got landed on a London and South Western Railway train and eventually arrived at Waterloo Station. I felt a bit fed up about it, but it was good to be in Blighty. The country looked lovely on the train journey. France in parts looks beautiful, but it doesn't beat dear England. Well I was deposited in J1 ward, King George Hospital, Waterloo Road, London SE and here I am on August 16th rapidly getting better."

On recovery Corporal Arthur Cooper was not passed fit for active service, he finished the war in England on training duties with the rank of Acting Sergeant. Apart from finding out that Arthur Cooper came from 231, Selly Park Road, nothing else about him has come to light. I hope he had a long and happy life after the war.

6

PAYING THE PRICE

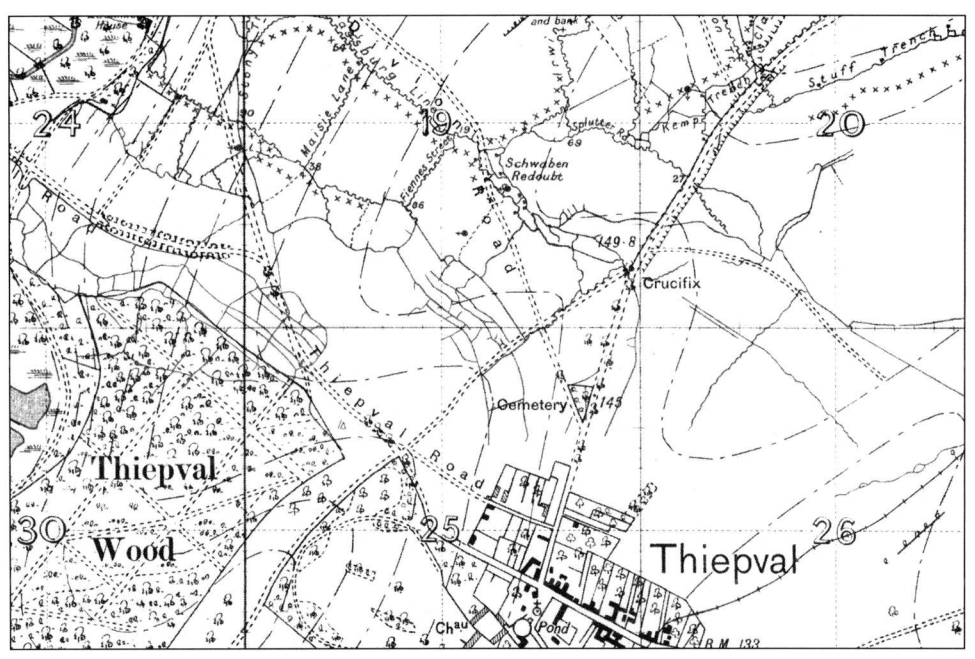

THE BARGAIN

It occurs to me that, when the call was made by country in the early days of the Great War and later by Kitchener, it was responded to by men from all walks of life. In the early days, inspired by thoughts of adventure and later, just by thoughts of doing one's duty. We read of tales of heroism and of awards for bravery, but what of the ordinary men from ordinary backgrounds and jobs who joined up, just to "do their bit"? There was nothing special about them, they joined to do what they had to do and, in so doing, many, many of them paid the ultimate price without heroics. They just disappeared from the face of the earth without making any great impact on life and leaving it similarly. This was the army made up of 'ordinary Joes'.

We cannot, after this length of time, find out much about them, save for their name being engraved on one of the many memorials to be found here on the Somme and at home. It could be, that many of them were not brave in the way it is traditionally known, they had led unremarkable lives and died unremarkable deaths, but, in so doing, they bought our future. They may have been terrified at the prospect of their ordeal but still went through with it. This poem reflects my thoughts on the ordinary soldiers, who were truly heroes and epitomise the saying, "Cometh the hour cometh the man".

THE BARGAIN

Where is he now, that child whose life was spent
Hiding in shadows, blending within a world of grey,
Thinking that soon his life might ebb away
Before his turn to joust within the tournament,
Yet hearing battle's call, light came into his eyes,
And he and all the others, newborn fledglings, came
To set alight a life, under the fires of French skies,
Not knowing it was they who, in the end, would feed its flame.

Now, in his passing, honour is satisfied,
The price is paid, from darkened halls to light he went,
The life he lived is over but he lies content,
A bargain struck and paid for in the instant that he died,
And in this sacrifice there is no recompense
For him who found himself, at last, and who
Requires no funeral march to bear him hence,
No, leave him sleeping peacefully, at rest, with other sons of Waterloo.

HOLLOW VICTORY

In many books on the Great War there is a photograph of, what is believed to be a skeletal German soldier, lying dead in what must be considered a distorted position. It is a truly horrific picture which portrays, for me, all the grim reality of this conflict.

I am always mindful that in walking these fields I am actually entering the largest cemetery in Europe. It is very easy to walk on a summer's day, following old footsteps, engrossed in my friends' accounts of the military action which took place in a particular area, to forget that, just below the surface, lie many remains which will probably never be recovered for proper burial.

This poem, inspired by a wet afternoon walk in the area known as White City, is trying to portray that death is in no way glorious. The act of dying may be considered so, but after that, all that remains is what may be thought of as rubbish. Most of this area is fertilised by the remains of the fallen, so in seeing its undoubted beauty, we are also witnessing a rebirth of sorts. So we, who share in this beauty, may gain some consolation, but, in so doing, we also carry with us the burden of knowledge, that our ability to visit these places was bought at such a terrible cost.

HOLLOW VICTORY

Arms crossed, in vain attempt to cover his dead face,
The conquering army treads, uncaring, over him.
He lies, unnoticed, frozen in his falling place,
And is long gone, he travels far over the rim
Of that dark valley segregating living from the dead,
He lies, as garbage, cast aside,
While those who live, to victory forge ahead,
He should be there to share their joy, but he just died.

Oh! We will try; we'll make our pitiful attempt,
With tears and lamentations to atone
For such a waste of life, such dreams undreamt,
And we will cover acres of his homeland with white stone,
Despite all this, we carry, heavy with disgrace,
The weight of arms, crossed, covering a dead face.

TIDES OF TRUTH

You have only to look at the magnificent Thiepval Memorial to grasp the enormity of the sacrifice made around this area. The 75,000 names on it are of those unfortunates who vanished from the face of the earth during the battles. All these lads, there one minute, gone the next, leaving no trace of their existence. The difficulty is, that many bodies were interred properly on death but further action then destroyed and obliterated their graves. Wounded men, without the strength to get back to home lines, lay in No Man's Land unable to be helped, until they either died of their wounds or were victims of the next artillery attack.

At the Sunken Road, near Beaumont Hamel, the Lancashire Fusiliers "jumped off" and marched slowly across the fields toward their objective. Faced with an unperceived eight foot drop, halfway there, the attack stalled and they were silhouetted against the skyline with the obvious result of carnage at the hands of machine guns firing from the outskirts of the village. The wounded could not get back and the fate described in my poem befell them.

What must the thoughts of the next line up have been, hearing the pitiful groans of those beyond their help? All that could be done was to wait for the inevitable end, in whatever way it came. The surviving troops knew that they had only survived because their mates had died. It would do no harm for us to remember that we too "swim on this eternal tide of men".

TIDES OF TRUTH

The truth is this, so use it as you will,
Putting aside the myth that tells of death as glory,
And all the other myths, extolling machines built to kill,
This is the truth, which in relaying tells a different story.

Know, that those hopes moulded throughout the years,
Fashioned into those ways we understood
Now lie destroyed, death the invader shouts our fears,
Destroying more than we can pay for with our blood.

Nothing in death is elegant, nor dying stately,
There is no beauty in what lived, and now lies shattered,
Here was a life, vibrant, alive till lately,
Filled with the many little things that mattered.

Out there he lies, a nuisance, life ebbing away,
While we are safe, listening, powerless to ease
His passing, save at the end to lay him down beneath the clay
He fought for, how does the Lord account for lives like these?

He should be counted high, his name held up in pride,
He who lies low be praised, his name revered and then
We who remain, who still have strength to battle with the tide,
Should know, we swim on this eternal tide of men.

LAST IMPRESSIONS

Humility is an English trait, we are, by nature, a fairly self effacing race and I believe, a fairly religious one. Not in the sense of churchgoing and formal worship, but in a deeply held inner belief that we are all the same and that we should, therefore, do as little harm to "the other chap" as possible. If I am right, how terrible it must have been to be cast into the maelstrom of the Somme battles.

I may be accused of dealing overlong with death in my poems, I make no apology, death was a constant companion in those dark days, with the watchword being "when", not "if". Why otherwise could a wound be so warmly welcomed? It meant respite from the constant threat and a chance to forget the horrors of circumstance for a while, if that were possible. The bravery of these men is that they were aware of this threat, accepted it and carried on.

I have tried with this poem, which I started in Mametz Wood, to create some sort of final prayer for someone who knew that very soon he may be among the dead, many of whom were his pals. His life thus far hadn't amounted to much, just an ordinary soldier who hoped that, with his sacrifice, might come entry into Heaven. I have no doubt that his hopes were realised.

LAST IMPRESSIONS

I hope today to enter heaven
And in this journey to my Lord,
Gain my reward for this God given
Chance to fall upon my sword.

I will tell him, "This life was passed
With little honour, in conceit,
Unworthy was I till the last
Of those who lie here at my feet".

Soon, I will join that brilliant band
Within the selflessness of death,
May this last action join our hands,
And take away my Saviour's breath.

EPITAPH

Mansell Copse Cemetery has always been my favourite spot to visit. The front line, two hundred yards behind this spot, is where the 8th and 9th Devonshires "jumped off" on 1st July 1916. They were mown down by machine gun fire and were buried here in, what had been, their original front line trench. The gateway to the cemetery contains an evocative stone tablet which says, "The Devonshires held this trench, the Devonshires hold it still". This cemetery contains the remains of another famous poet A E Hodgson who wrote the evocative poem "Before Battle", two days before he died, so it has a special interest for me.

What is not commonly known, is that one of their officers, Captain D L Martin, on leave prior to the attack, made a plasticine model of the land over which he was to lead his attack and predicted its demise by machine gun fire from a strong point which he knew existed in the civilian cemetery at Mametz. He was an experienced officer and knowing what awaited him and his men, he still led them bravely in the attack to his and their cost. I cannot imagine greater bravery than this. I know I could not have done it and this short poem is by way of a tribute to this man and those who served under him who are buried here. Mansell Copse Cemetery is well worth a visit. It is secluded, quiet and the outline of the trench in which these brave lads are laid is still visible in the trees at the far end. Visit this place and pay tribute to them, they are worth it.

EPITAPH

Here, I will die,

Folded within the heart of France; in the French sky
Above the larks flock homeward, silent as they fly,
The evening mist enfolds this place where tall trees were cut down
By winds of chance, green leaves discarded, withered, brown,
At home the lamps are dimmed and curtains drawn,
And frosted dewdrops create silver threads upon the lawn,
Smoke from summer bonfires hangs in English skies,
And England joins with France here where I lie.

CRUCIFIX CORNER

On the road passing through Bazentin Ridge, near to Longueval, are the two villages of Bazentin le Grand and Bazentin le Petit. In this vicinity the loss of life was immense. On one day in August 1916, the 33rd Battalion Machine Gun Corps allegedly fired one million rounds over High Wood approximately one mile away, thereby preventing German reserves forming up to reinforce their front line. In a little wooded copse, at the side of the road, is a battle scarred life sized crucifix which was in place before this terrible time and survived, virtually intact. The figure of Christ bears the marks of his original suffering and additional marks from this awful period in history. I find it hard to believe that this statue has endured, but I guess we have to believe, as Christians, that the love of Christ is forever and this reminder of Christ's sacrifice seems to bear witness to that, even though it shows the ravages of war. My difficulty, however, is that we continue to commit all kinds of atrocities in the name of whatever religion we purport to follow.

Being a simple man, I believe in treating others as I would expect to be treated, but standing at this spot in the fields of Picardy, I have great difficulty in reconciling the events which took place here with my philosophy. How could a loving God, whose son is represented by this statue, allow this terrible carnage? But, then I think that this statue has looked on as the most terrible events have unfurled here. It is still here, as is the love of God. It is us who choose to ignore it and "go our own way", often with disastrous results, the results of which, are still evident in this part of France.

CRUCIFIX CORNER

Bodies hanging, gleaming white,
Where the skylarks wheel and dive,
Rotting in the warm sunlight,
Once were bright, young and alive.

Bodies piling, yellow, black,
Rotting in the summer light,
Teeth laid bare, lips curling back,
As each tortured soul took flight.

Limbs distorted by the fight,
Other horrors, worse by far,
Come into the mind at night,
Stretched by madness, torn by war.

Jesus hanging from a tree,
Crucified upon a cross,
Surely men must brothers be?
Or your death is mankind's loss.

WHY?

The Great War was the first one to be witnessed, due to the new 'miracle' of cinematography, by those who waited at home. There had been footage of previous conflicts but this was the first to receive such comprehensive coverage. The film "The Battles of the Somme and the Ancre" were the first 'spectaculars' to reach home cinemas and were thought to be so horrific in parts that women fainted.

Thus, the cinematographers brought home the horrors of what was being suffered by our troops but only partially, as there was no sound and no film can reflect first hand experience any more than television today can reflect the horrors of modern conflict.

But what of the cinematographers themselves? They, from a distance, could witness the slaughter, experience the fear, hear the sounds and smell the stench of death. They had no knowledge of war, yet they were to record its horror for posterity. Much of the footage which was shot did not see the light of day at the time. Propaganda was as much part of this war as any other. Footage, or even photographs, of dead allied soldiers were not permitted to be shown at home. The whole object of such films was, as always, to show glorious victories, won by smiling soldiers.

Hawthorn Ridge is the scene of the detonation of a mine. Footage of this event is featured in many films on the Great War and in all of those relating to the Battles of the Somme. Whilst standing on the spot where Lieutenant Geoffrey Malins was standing when he shot his, now famous, footage of this event in a place of horror where many died in the early morning of 1st July 1916, I was struck by the thought of what might have been his reaction, as he witnessed those events taking place before his lens and eyes? With a little artistic licence this poem is trying to reflect those thoughts.

WHY?

See how they fall, as leaves fall from a tree
In autumn, in the chill of afternoon.
There was no wind, no gust, save to eternity,
But silently they fell like shadows 'cross the moon
And in the morning light I watch, carefully as they
Still fall and now the silent, withered, lay
Struck by no hand of God, nor pestilence,
I watch demanding of this, "Where is the sense
Of men melting like raindrops into chalk and clay?"

TERRY CARTER ON "PAYING THE PRICE"

Having visited the battlefields several times with Paul, I know that there is one cemetery which is one of his favourite places to visit. Its official name is the 'Devonshire Cemetery, Mametz.' This cemetery is in a small wood, on the ridge of a slope, just off the main road. The wood was given the name Mansel Copse probably after the death of Second Lieutenant SLM Mansel-Carey of the 9th Devons who was mortally wounded by a German rifle grenade in the remains of the copse (we are talking of a few shattered tree stumps only) whilst supervising a working-party in February 1916.

It is very hard to get orientated whilst in the cemetery as it is surrounded by trees and the drop to the road below is quite steep. Because the cemetery was originally part of the front trench system you automatically get the impression that the advance at zero hour on the 1st July, 1916, took place with the Devons crossing the main road in the direction of Mametz. However, this is not so, the Devons advance across No Man's Land took them alongside the road towards the distant village of Fricourt.

Another fact which may surprise some, is that this is not the trench that the Devons formed up in prior to advancing across No Man's Land. The front and reserve line trenches at Mansel Copse were in a prime location for German artillery and became so badly damaged that a new trench, which was known as 'New Trench', was dug 250 yards behind Mansel Copse. Luckily the Germans did not know this and on the morning of the 1st July, prior to the attack, German artillery bombarded the old front line trenches. This would have caused considerable casualties if our troops had, in fact, been manning them.

As Paul has mentioned, Captain Duncan Martin's prediction, regarding the advance, proved correct. There was a German machine-gun strong-point situated near the crucifix in the civilian cemetery in Mametz. The 9th Devons were designated to be the first wave on a frontage of 400 yards with Captain Martin's 1 Company on the right and 2 Company on the left.

At 7:30am on the 1st July the 9th Devons climbed out of 'New Trench' and formed up to advance towards the German front line opposite. It took around four minutes to reach the shell ravaged front line in Mansel Copse. They then had to negotiate the downward shell cratered and barbed wire strewn slope into No Man's Land. The German machine-gun strongpoint had survived the British artillery barrage and deadly enfiladed machine-gun fire of 450 rounds per minute cut the right hand company down like a scythe. Captain Martin was mortally wounded leading his company into the 'Danger Spot' in which he had predicted.

Later in the day they returned to bury their dead, 123 men of the 9th Devons and thirty-eight of the 8th Devons, in a section of their old front line trench in Mansel Copse. The mass grave was then marked by their famous sign:

THE DEVONSHIRES HELD THIS TRENCH: THE DEVONSHIRES HOLD IT STILL.

This famous motto is now inscribed in a stone tablet near the entrance to the cemetery.

This aspect of the Somme battlefields, that of burying the dead, has always been of interest to me as, in the heat of battle and its immediate aftermath, thoughts of Christian burial may have been cast aside. However, when things quietened down, I am sure every effort was made to honour those who had fallen, by granting them wherever possible this basic Christian rite, as shown by the survivors of the Devonshires.

In this respect, I should now like to move onto a cemetery in Caterpillar Valley which Paul has previously referred to and which gave him the inspiration for this poem, "The Little Chap".

Flatiron Copse Cemetery came into being a couple of weeks or so, after the successful attack launched against the Bazentin –Longueval Ridge that began at dawn on the 14th July 1916, this area being taken by troops of the 3rd and 7th Divisions. After this attack, the German front line was pushed back to a new trench known as the 'Switch Line' that ran in front of Martinpuich, through the northern corner of High Wood, skirting the village of Flers and meandering onwards towards Combles. This resulted in the British front line from Bazentin le Petit – High Wood – Longueval forming a salient and German artillery being able to fire on it from three sides. The low ground running along Caterpillar Valley towards the quarry on the northern edge of Bernafay Wood and the low ground running alongside Mametz Wood passing Flatiron copse and Sabot Copse were areas that German artillery would pound with continuous shellfire day and night. The track making its way along past Flatiron Copse became one of the main arterial routes to keep the front line supplied with men, food, water, equipment and ammunition.

One can only guess at the scene along this valley. Shattered and smashed gun-limbers, transport wagons, both British and German and the dead of both sides strewn everywhere. To some troops it was known as "Dead-Horse Valley", however the name "Death Valley", which was the name by which it became known, was, no doubt, more appropriate.

Possibly, the area opposite Flatiron Copse suffered from less German artillery fire than other areas and, for that reason, an advanced dressing station was established there. As with all dressing stations, a cemetery was always an obligatory addition, thus, Flatiron Copse Cemetery was formed on the sloping ground opposite the copse.

The original 400 graves in the cemetery are all in Plot 1 near the main entrance, with all the graves behind the Stone of Remembrance being the last resting place of remains brought in from smaller cemetery sites, as they were closed and from further battlefield clearances of the neighbouring area.

As Paul has previously mentioned, the cemetery contains the grave of 20 year old Mons veteran Corporal Edward Dwyer V.C. who served in the 1st Bn. East Surrey Regiment. Fulham born and bred, Edward Dwyer joined up in 1913 at the age of 17 and had won the Victoria Cross within two years. His records note how, while under fire from scores of German soldiers on "Hill 60" in Ypres, Belgium, he stood up and threw hand grenades at the enemy. All the other British troops around him had been killed but Pte Dwyer fought until he, too, was badly wounded. At the time, he was the youngest soldier in the British Army to receive the VC and, as a result, became a celebrity back home in Fulham, where the War Office decided to use his achievement for propaganda purposes. Back in Britain, he made a record in which he talked with great enthusiasm of his experiences at the front and gave a rousing rendition of the soldiers' classic song, "We're here because we're here".

Dwyer was sent out in a recruiting role and persuaded hundreds of young men to enlist. However, a less savoury side of his character is also revealed in his military records. It is noted that Pte Dwyer was punished for stealing another soldier's boots, though apparently someone else had taken his. Like so many of his courageous generation, languishing at home was not to Pte Dwyer's liking. While recruiting in London, he was itching to get back into the fight and persuaded his superiors to return him to the front.

On 2nd September, 1916, the 1st East Surrey's (95th Brigade, 5th Division) were in the reserve trenches at Maltz Horn Farm and the following day Edward was killed when the 1st East Surrey's were in support during the attack between Guillemont and Wedge Wood.

Another sad, but interesting, fact about Flatiron Copse Cemetery is that it contains three sets of brothers who are buried together. Ernest and Herbert Philby of the Middlesex Regiment, who died of gas poisoning whilst their battalion was sheltering in Mametz Wood on 21st August, 1916, the Hardwidge brothers of the 15th Welsh (Carmarthenshire) and the Tregaskis brothers who were both Lieutenants in the 16th Welsh (Cardiff City Battalion).

Another young officer buried in the cemetery is Second Lieutenant E J Pusch of the 11th Royal Warwicks, who died on 8th August, 1916. His elder brother, Frederick Pusch DSO of the 1st Bn. Irish Guards was killed seven weeks earlier at Ypres and is buried in Essex Farm Cemetery.

On looking in the cemetery register you will find that on approximately half of the 1,522 graves the soldiers' ages are unknown, but, of those whose ages are recorded, two were mere boys of sixteen years old. They were Privates George William Fleming of the Suffolk Regiment, killed on 15th July, 1916 and T Griffin of the Royal Irish Fusiliers who is named on the Special Memorial. As Paul has indicated, this cemetery is, probably more than some of the others, certainly a place of real memory and a place where, whilst Paul was compelled to write his poem about Corporal Dwyer, as he was when he was killed, I could swear I could hear the soft refrain carried on the wind, "We're here because we're here, because we're here, because we're here".

Paul has his own particular favourite spots on the Somme, and so too, do I.

My own particular favourite is the area surrounding High Wood and I have read many Divisional and Battalion histories that were published after WW1 concerning the actions that took place in and around it from 14th July to 15th September 1916. However it was one particular comment in the "History of the 51st (Highland) Division" that instilled me with a strong desire to make a more serious investigation. The author made the following comment concerning the area around High Wood at the end of the war:

"High Wood stands in the centre of a vast cemetery. There is barely a portion of ground of the size of a tennis court in all that countryside which does not contain the grave of one or more British soldiers."

Over the years I have walked tracks and fields near High Wood many, many times and even now it is hard to imagine what the post-war scene must have looked with its shell blasted landscape. The only visible remains of High Wood, a few shell splintered tree trunks no more than a few feet tall, the entire landscape scattered with wooden crosses indicating individual or multiple burials. To help me understand more I contacted the Headquarters of the Commonwealth War Graves Commission located in Maidenhead. As a result I was given permission to visit their HQ and was able to view the original cemetery indexes created, at the end of the war, by the, then Army run, "Graves Registration Units" which were the forerunners of the Commonwealth War Graves Commission. These units cleared the battlefields during the immediate post-war years.

I was interested in viewing the original cemetery index for Caterpillar Valley Cemetery, as this is what is known as, a Concentration Cemetery.

Originally Caterpillar Valley Cemetery was created for the burials of men belonging to the 38th (Welsh) Division who were killed around 28th August 1918. Twenty-five casualties from the 38th Division were buried in Caterpillar Valley Cemetery. In fact, whoever gave the Cemetery its name must have got his bearings wrong. Caterpillar Valley is a few hundreds yards distant behind the Cemetery. A more apt name would have been Bazentin Ridge Cemetery or Green Dump Cemetery (Green Dump was an area just behind the cemetery. It was the rendezvous point for some of the Tanks and a stockpile for their fuel and ammunition, prior to the very first Tank action on 15th September 1916).

During the battlefield clearances at the end of the war it was decided to make Caterpillar Valley Cemetery a concentration cemetery to where the bodies interred in the graves, previously mentioned in the 51st Highland Division History, were transferred.

Those bodies that were found were dug up and re-buried in Caterpillar Valley. Thus from the original twenty-five burials (which nowadays is Plot 1 in the cemetery) the cemetery became the second largest cemetery on the Somme battlefield with 5,569 burials. Nigh on 4,000 of these graves are "Unknown Soldiers" and quite a few of those who are identified came from the many of smaller battlefield cemeteries from around Bazentin le Grand and Le Petit, High Wood and even as far as Flers. The following are some of the Cemeteries that were closed and from where the remains recovered from their graves were transferred to Caterpillar Valley Cemetery:

CLARK'S DUMP CEMETERY, BAZENTIN, was a little West of High Wood, on the road from Bazentin-le-Petit to Flers. It contained the graves of 26 soldiers from the United Kingdom, and two from South Africa, who fell in August-December, 1916.

GINCHY GERMAN CEMETERY (500 yards North of the village, between the Flers and Lesboeufs roads), in which two unknown British soldiers were buried.

McCORMICK'S POST CEMETERY, FLERS, nearly a mile West of Flers village. Here were buried 19 soldiers from the United Kingdom, nine from Australia and nine from New Zealand, who fell in September-November, 1916.

MARTINPUICH ROAD CEMETERY, BAZENTIN, containing the graves of 41 soldiers from the United Kingdom who fell in July and August, 1916.

SNOWDON CEMETERY, BAZENTIN, in Bazentin-Ie-Grand village, containing the graves of 24 soldiers of the 38th (Welsh) Division who fell in August and September, 1918.

WELSH CEMETERY, LONGUEVAL, between Flers village and High Wood, in which were buried 17 soldiers of the 38th (Welsh) Division who fell in August and September, 1918.

FLERS ROAD CEMETERY situated on the Longueval to Flers Road approximately half a mile south of Flers.

FLERS DRESSING STATION CEMETERY situated on Longueval to Flers Road about one mile south of Flers.

HIGHLAND CEMETERY, HIGH WOOD, situated on the Longueval to Martinpuich Road adjacent to High Wood and around 400 yards before the present day London Cemetery.

BLACK WATCH CEMETERY, HIGH WOOD, situated on the farm track that runs from the Southern corner of High Wood to Crucifix Corner near Bazentin le Petit. Approximately 400 yards south of High Wood.

CROSS ROADS CEMETERY, BAZENTIN, situated at the cross road junction of the road running from Bazentin le Grand to Bazentin le Petit opposite Crucifix Corner.

After the war, sections of men belonging to the Graves Registration Units searched areas of the former battlefields for graves with markers in addition to areas with tell tale signs of where other bodies may have been buried. Using the area around High Wood as an example, areas of ground were taped off into fifty yard squares that corresponded with a trench map and a group of men would slowly walk across the ground. Wooden crosses marked many a grave but there were also several other signs to indicate that a body lay buried in an unmarked grave. Grass or crops grew stronger over remains and puddles over them had a bluish tinge. Rat holes with human bones, human remains and equipment littered the ground and were self evident. It must have been grim work at the time, but the system worked otherwise, there would not have been over 5000 bodies transferred to Caterpillar Valley Cemetery.

The original cemetery index for Caterpillar Valley Cemetery, which I was allowed to research, gives the map reference of where the bodies were found on the battlefields to within a fifty yard square. I made a note of all these positions and built up a data base.

On a Trench Map, High Wood stands in squares 4a, 4b, 4c, and 4d. I discovered that nearly 900 bodies which were reburied in Caterpillar Valley Cemetery were found during the post-war battlefield searches in these four squares. The majority of them were found in the confines of High Wood itself. South of High Wood in the land adjacent to Martinpuich - Longueval Road and across the field towards Wood Lane around another 800 remains were unearthed. A sobering thought, when walking in the vicinity of High Wood, is that, apart from standing in an area which was so much fought over that it once resembled a lunar landscape criss-crossed with trenches, it was also one vast cemetery for men whose only legacy now, is their name inscribed onto the Thiepval Memorial, so that "We shall remember them".

7

AFTERMATH

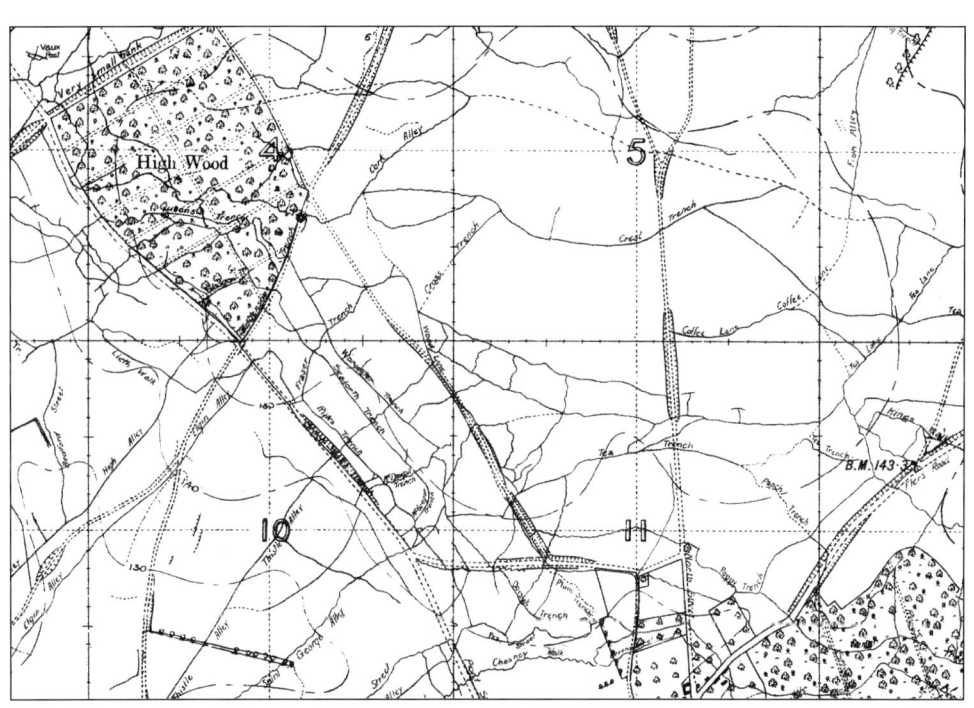

BROKEN

I cannot fail to wonder, on my walks, how, in such a small area, so many lives were lost, so many bodies broken and so many minds destroyed. It is impossible to walk around the areas of the Ancre without being struck by the sheer volume of cemeteries and crosses. These are marking only the resting places of those who were recovered, how many sleep beneath our feet is still unknown.

I have, as a result of my experiences in this area, started to question whether there is anything in the world worth killing another human being for. When I was younger this was "just the way it was". The Second World War had just ended and I had acquired the view that war was a necessary evil, without fully grasping its reality. The reality I now see, is that people's lives are ended, their bodies and their minds are broken prematurely. Surely nothing can support this tragedy.

This poem seeks to explore my changing view. We all have optimistic hopes, these are often dashed, but we don't get killed or physically hurt as a result.

When you consider the change in the perspectives of the Great War from 1914 to 1916, I think you may get the idea. Enthusiasm changed to disenchantment, these feelings mirror my own evolution of thought on war over the years.

The area which I walk and the number of casualties sustained in it, was gradually instrumental in cementing the view in the minds of our soldiers and those of our people at home, that this was not the great adventure it had originally been promoted to be. It was needless carnage, no advantage, no gain. Walk the front line positions of 1st July 1916 to the final positions of November, and consider what lies beneath your feet. Was this "gain" worth it?

BROKEN

Where once strong fingers reached to grasp the clouds
And sinews strained, in vain attempt to touch the sun,
Now, all lies withered, part of a broken crowd,
Drowned in this stagnant pool of life part run.

Where once, in hope eternal, sprang the sapling strong
And resolute, upon the tallest bough, the highest of them all,
Drab birds now perch, breaking its branches, hurling them headlong
Into decay, returning them to earth stunted and small.

Despair and helplessness announce a life's disease
And callously reveal, in curtain call
The sky of hope may easily be touched in peace,
The broken boughs of war cause us to fall.

REFLECTION

This poem was inspired by the same walk as the previous one and written at nearly the same time. I was looking through the perimeter fence of High Wood and caught a glimpse of a pool, which I now know to be a crater. It was a time of real intensity of feeling for me. I had considered all those who were killed, injured or broken in the poem of that name, but what of those who escaped unscathed, if it is possible to put it like that?

They would return home, after experiences which would make young men into old men overnight. Whatever youth they had looked forward to had gone, along with their hopes and aspirations. How could this cost be counted in the ever-growing casualty lists? These lads simply grew old before their time as a result of what they had seen and been called on to do. The simple task of shaving would cause them to look in the mirror and what face would look back at them? I imagined the same faces in later life, gazing into a pool just as I was. What thoughts would go round their head? Would they like what they saw? Probably not. A life full of hope, wasted, through no doing of their own. So if you don't like what you see in the pool, drop a pebble and the reflection disappears . . . . . but it always comes back!

REFLECTION

By a silent silver mirror, hidden from inhuman race,
Sitting there, looking within, reflected back I saw a face,
Not one careworn, tired and haggard; younger, fresher, full of fun,
Knowing nothing of tomorrow, life was mine, my race to run,
Dreams disrupted by a madness changed into reality,
Face returned with every horror etching its maturity,
Gone, the simple hope of childhood, flown on wings of might have been,
Disappeared the strength of youth, spent in the years of in-between,
Manhood's wisdom passed me by upon my road from then to now,
Contentment in maturity, eluded me somehow,
Oh! How I hate my alter ego mocking down the years at me,
Drop a pebble, watch the ripples, no reflection now to see.

SURVIVORS?

The names of the dead, so far as they are known, are listed for all to see, in the various cemetery and memorial record books which abound on the Somme Battlefields. It is right that this is so, because those who are named within them sacrificed all for their country. In paying respects to these brave souls in these tranquil spots, I am often struck by the thought that many, many of the lads were so terribly wounded that they may, in the light of events when they returned home, have secretly wished that they, too, had been killed. I am not referring to those "lucky enough" to have received a "Blighty One" (a wound which was serious enough to ensure repatriation for a while, but which was not life threatening in itself). No, I am talking about those poor souls who suffered serious injury, amputation or perhaps the gas victims, all of whom carried with them lasting results on their future quality of life. Wilfred Owen sums the plight of these most unfortunate "survivors" in his excellent poem "Disabled".

If we add to their suffering the fact that, despite all previous promises, there were no "homes for heroes" and no jobs for soldiers who had been disabled. They were, therefore, reduced to menial tasks such as selling matches, which carried with it an element of charity and the feelings of pity which would, no doubt, have been felt by those who came into contact with those so terribly injured.

There are many excellent charities which have sprung up since the Great War, all dedicated to giving loving and compassionate care to its casualties, but, I believe that the seriously wounded were, previously, independent, strong men, reduced to their pitiful state only through serving their country. I cannot believe that, if I were in this position, I would be grateful to anyone for this kind of "survival".

SURVIVORS?

When it is over, count well within the cost
Those broken by war, more numerous than the slain,
Those who, in "winning", gave part of themselves and lost,
Their sacrifice concealed within "the greater gains".

They will return "triumphant" to their homeland cities
Where healing hands will mend and tend the pain,
Their lives to be endured, broken objects of pity,
Within those crippled frames their captive agile brains.

There will be hollow empty voices calling
For "work for heroes"; those who carry on their vain
Attempt at self support are helpless, falling
Head first into the mud, soaked by the unrelenting rain.

What has been sacrificed is gone and in its giving
That which made man stand tall will not be seen again,
The dead are gone, the half alive continue "living"
And wish that they had fallen with the slain.

THE PLACE IN THE LINE

This poem was inspired by my visits to the Somme, but not by anywhere in particular. It was also inspired by my son, who I don't see too often, as he lives in Ireland and works as a pilot. I enjoy his company immensely and even though they have happened many times, our partings are always tinged with sadness. But I am lucky! How many fathers have said goodbye to sons who have never returned and lived their life with regret at things they might have said, had they known. It is now commonplace for demonstrations of affection between fathers and sons, but I have the feeling that in 1916 things were not like that, sons went off to do their duty, dads were proud, but didn't say so and mums wept silently.

This poem was quite easy, I had only to think how I would feel if, God forbid, my son was taken from me. It may seem strange to say that it was easy, but this is one of the few poems in this book that I can say I have written with a first hand view. I know what I feel for my son, I know how I would feel if he wasn't there. I hope I have captured these feelings and that nothing has been lost in their transposition into another time.

THE PLACE IN THE LINE

We walked in the fading sunset awhile,
My soldier boy and I,
We laughed at the pleasure of each passing mile
Spent beneath the darkening sky,
But laughter hid only the emptiness
Of the words that we both left unsaid,
Then he hurried back to his place in the line
And I to my welcoming bed
And the pain of my tears left unshed,

Never shall I share the good times again
With that young man who so mirrored me,
The future which beckoned calls to me in vain,
For that future will now never be,
The madness has taken a life which was mine,
Cast it down in the pit, dark and deep,
Where my son lies at rest in his place in the line
And his father lies waiting for sleep
And the strength to just break down and weep.

DOGS OF WAR

This poem was not really inspired by walking the battlefields of the Somme, rather as a result of it. My interest in the Great War is well known to my family, who have seen it escalate from a passing interest in 1995 to a genuine thirst for knowledge and understanding nearly ten years later. I do gain a lot of such understanding from associating with and walking alongside people like Terry Carter whose knowledge of the actual battles and regiments involved on the Somme, it is, on one hand, very enlightening, but, on the other, I cannot begin to comprehend how he remembers it all!

As a result of my son Matt's marriage to Susan, I now have an extended family and many friends in Southern Ireland. These long suffering people are also now saddled with and probably bored by, my interest.

It is not too well known that many Irish regiments fought by our side in 1914-1918 and, on discussing this aspect one night with a dear Irish friend, he informed me that many of the Irish officers left behind their packs of hounds when they joined up into, presumably, cavalry regiments. This painted a picture to me of what happened to these packs. Were they looked after? Or did they just fade away pining for their masters? I don't know the answer, but these questions inspired this poem.

DOGS OF WAR

What of the brave, who rode away
To hunt for the fox in fields of grey,
Who, in their fences overleaping
Fell to the earth and now lie sleeping
In ditches swathed in battle red,
Now sleep awhile and now are dead,
While faithful friends wait in green pastures
Reunion, with absent masters,
Silent, yet questioning they scan
Each day's horizon, for their man
Who heard the call and took to horse
Falling, e'er he had run his course,
Scarce knowing what he had died for,
Leaving behind, these dogs of war.
Shall these mute victims of his chase
Add casualties to war's disgrace?
Or will the passing of their days
Be witness to the better way?

BELIEF

There is a well known poem entitled "The Soldier's Poem" and I make no apologies for using that fine piece as a basis for "Belief". It occurred to me on a visit to Bapaume Post cemetery on the outskirts of Albert, which contains the remains of the Second Lieutenant William Furse from Birmingham, that, due to the decision that all combatants would be buried where they fell, or in close proximity and that no remains would be transported home, there would only be a very limited opportunity, if any, for mothers, wives, sweethearts, fathers, brothers, or any family or friend to visit the grave of a loved one. This, I believe, is a fundamental part of the grieving process, and one which is more recognised today.

I fully understand the reasoning behind this earlier ruling and of course, casualty figures were so appallingly high as preclude transportation to and internment at home. Nevertheless, there were many left at home to cope with their loss in the absence of a "grieving place". Is this what their loved ones died for? What message might they have for their families?

I wrote this poem to try and answer that question, by attempting to visualise the thoughts of one of the many fallen. At least with a grave there is closure, without one there is only memory. Those left behind in such circumstances must have been very, very strong people.

I hope this poem will also help anyone who has suffered the grief of loss of a loved one. If it does, I believe I may have not only succeeded in my original aim, but brought comfort of the past into the present, and I will be content.

BELIEF

You may ask me, "Why did you leave
Me behind here, alone to grieve?"
But listen to me as I say,
"We are not parted by today,
Closer are we than you can know,
You'll hear me in the winds that blow
And in each silver shower of rain
I will stand by your side again,
From now until eternity
I'll be with you and you with me,
Do not stay here, no, do not cry,
What we had . . . that will never die,
Do not feel sorrow, do not grieve,
From this day on, please, just believe".

FLOWERS

I have previously mentioned the many, many cemeteries which lie on or near the old battlefields. Some are large, some are small, but all have one thing in common, they are "pieces of England" on French soil. The land was granted in perpetuity by the French to England after the Great War.

Another pleasing aspect of these peaceful places is that, thanks to the magnificent work of worthy souls, the cemeteries are immaculately presented and tended. This must be a great comfort to those who visit the last resting place of a loved one and each grave contains a small planted area where typical English flowers are planted and tended.

I was considering these flowers, at the Sucerie Cemetery just off the Serre Road, when it occurred to me that most of the lads would have looked forward to parcels from home, as a small reminder of normality and of the cause for which they were fighting. The everyday things which we now take for granted must have seemed very precious to them. If you read, as I do, the letters sent home, by them, to their loved ones, it is clear that the writers did not tell their relatives the full story of what it was like for them at the front. I think they thought that any sacrifices they made would make for a better life for those at home and in return, if the worst came, was it too much to ask that the flowers of home that marked their spot were tended lovingly? I don't think so and my sincere thanks go to the many good souls who work for the Commonwealth War Graves Commission and who do so much caring work on our behalf.

FLOWERS

The light is bright and I am young and there is no more pain,
I have returned to days before, when youthful songs were sung,
Those times, long gone, I never thought ever to see again,
When I was older than my years and you were very young,
For you the sun will shine again, within its light you'll see
The days I purchase here for you, with this poor life the fee,
Each day thus bought, so full of hope, a time where life will be
Even in your solitude, counted as spent with me,
For me, the sun kissed flowers will dance and sway above my place,
My sunrise melts into the clay its destiny untasted,
I shall not fear the darkness, where no sun touches my face,
My little life is sacrificed, but it will not be wasted,
If, by this price your peace is won, then I am fully paid
And more, if you will tend the flowers that dance where I am laid.

MEMORIAL

In walking the battlefields of the Somme, you cannot fail to be moved and I have to say, impressed by the quantity of small cemeteries and the care with which they are tended. The small cemeteries are usually close to a particular action, whilst the larger ones have usually resulted from the re-internment, after the war, of the remains from some of the smaller ones and then, of course, there are those who, due to the ferocity and movement of war, have no graves, simply because they are still within the fields or because they no longer exist as an entity. These souls are remembered on the large memorials like the magnificent one at Thiepval.

Regardless of the location of their remembrance, the splendid work of tending the land, granted in perpetuity by France to England, goes on and they are places of great beauty and peace.

It is a shame that, to a degree, the same care is not apparent in England. Many of the smaller memorials have gone, some of the larger ones are not maintained. This is sad and I cannot help but reflect on the differences, which caused me to write this poem. Stand at Thiepval or Serre Road No.2 cemetery for a while. When you return home and compare, you will see what I mean.

MEMORIAL

They are not coming home, their silent names unanswered, lost,
They, who in morning sun leapt up, by noon lay down, lay dead,
Survivors send, in hollow tones, dread tidings of war's cost
To the villages which bore them from the beet fields where they bled.
Whisperings in dark houses, blinds now drawn against the day,
The low moans of lamentation echo two hundred miles away
From dead villages, new convents, with no men, all lost, all gone,
Not a father for the children, no soldier to cry upon.
See the ploughshare lying silent, empty inns devoid of sons,
Male voice choirs sang their finales far from where they once belonged.
Where unborn lives, ungenerated, lie rotting in the stench
Of wasted flesh, futures aborted in a shattered trench,
They will not rule, nor paint, nor shall they ever till the soil,
All that might be, is sacrificed, all nature's plans lie foiled
And all that lived lies silent, dead, by granite slab replaced,
For nature, time and common hand, their memory to erase.

LEGACY

This poem was borne out of frustration, at what I see as my inability to make people understand, by my poems and writings, the sheer enormity of what happens in wars generally and what has happened in this area of Picardy in particular. Each time I write a poem, I review and revise it until I cannot make it any better but still, to me, there is always something missing. If I was a photographer or an artist it might be easier, but all I would have produced is a picture. What I am seeking to portray are feelings, images of the soul, so to speak. The real frustration is in having to try to complement my work by writing a short piece about it. This practice is considered, by those cleverer than I, to be superfluous, as the words of a poem, according to them, should be self explanatory. Reading some of their obscure work, I am not so sure!

If you stand at Thiepval you cannot do other than wonder whether all the sacrifice was worthwhile. The answer is probably, that it was, because it was made by choice and out of altruism. However, since studying this period and standing at this spot a few times, I have become increasingly convinced that nothing is worth the taking of a life.

I wrote this poem as a warning to future generations about the folly of any repetition of their forefather's mistakes. I hope and pray they listen!

LEGACY

I try in vain to recreate a bygone scene,
Paint vivid pictures, images on a screen,
Moments of terror caught in time, a frightened face,
All must be painted; all must have a place,
So that my seed who follow me, daughters and sons
Will never search for truth within the sound of guns,
I, who can only seek to guide them with these sorry notes
Hope that their words of war will stick within their throats.

TERRY CARTER ON "AFTERMATH"

This group of poems all reflect the tremendous sense of loss felt by those at home, on hearing of their loved one's demise and of those who, in serving their country, sustained such injury as to affect them for the rest of their lives. Paul's writing causes me to consider that I have two sons of my own, at the time of writing the elder is 22 and the younger 19, and the thought of losing them, in war or peace, is unbearable. Yet nearly 800,000 British sons died during World War One. One cannot imagine the grief caused to probably, every family in the land as someone in their family circle died or was seriously wounded.

Looking at the local newspapers of the period you can see how proud some families were when all the male members of a particular family enlisted. It seemed to be a competition, who could boast the largest amount of men from one family to enlist! The Birmingham Weekly Post featured these family groups quite often and, no doubt, other papers did similarly the length and breadth of the country. Then, at the end of the war, the press showed photographs of family groups, with all the men coming through the war unscathed, an unusual phenomenon!

However, the saddest things that I found looking at the local press of the time were the columns dedicated to the 'missing'. Parents, brothers, sisters, wives and sweethearts asking for information regarding soldiers that were posted as missing. These requests carried on well after the war had finished. Some parents would not let go of the thought that their missing loved one might still turn up. Apparently, after the war thousands of former soldiers were in mental hospitals or in hospitals so badly disfigured that the authorities did not know their names!

Regarding the tremendous sense of loss felt by those at home, I feel I must draw the reader's attention to a couple of graves in Dartmoor Cemetery, Becordel-Becourt, not far from Albert on the Somme. It is hard to imagine the grief felt by a Mrs Frances Lee of London when she received two telegrams from the War Office notifying her of the death of her husband, 44 year old Sergeant George Lee and the other of her son, 19 year old Corporal Robert Lee. Both served in 'A' Battery 156th Brigade, Royal Field Artillery. They were killed together, on 5th September, 1916, in the same incident (German artillery fire) and lie buried next to each other.

The loss of such loved ones must have been terrible to bear for those left behind, but I am mindful of those unfortunate souls who returned home mentally and physically scarred and wounded. Even those who had escaped "unscathed" carried with them, for life, the memory of what they had seen, heard and experienced. Paul's poems "Broken", "Reflection" and

"Survivors?" reflect this terrible aspect of war. He has also mentioned in "Dogs of War" the innocent victims from the animal kingdom. Consider, if you will, the country's horses, mules, dogs, etc, sacrificed in this unspeakable horror.

Paul also mentions how well tended the Somme cemeteries are. For this we have to thank the Commonwealth War Graves Commission whose Headquarters are in Maidenhead. But, a massive thank you must also go to the Commission's gardens and maintenance staff. During my travels to the Somme over many years I have visited some cemeteries well off the beaten track that do not receive visitors for months on end, yet they are immaculate. The grass is cut, plants are in flower and there are no weeds. In October 2004, Paul and I, together with a couple of regular visitors to the Somme, stopped off on the way down. We visited Lapugnoy Cemetery a few miles from the town of Bethune. Whether it was a testament to my lack of map reading skills or it was a genuine 'out of the way' cemetery, it took ages to find it! We did, however, eventually discover it alongside a farm tractor track. Lapugnoy is a long narrowish cemetery with the graves, on a downward slope from the main entrance, surrounded by many trees. As you can guess, being October, the orange and bronze fallen leaves were thick on the ground.

According to the cemetery register there had been quite a gap since anyone else had visited. However, parked alongside the cemetery was a large white van belonging to a group of gardeners from the Commonwealth War Graves Commission. Apart from tending the flowers and weeding between the grave stones, they were cutting the grass and with the aid of air blowers they were blowing the dead leaves onto a large section of tarpaulin, which they then filled and rolled up with the leaves inside.

When the gardeners left, Lapugnoy Cemetery was in a beautiful state. Our thanks go to those five gardeners and all the rest in France and Belgium who work so hard and give 100% in tending the graves of our fallen.

It is their magnificent work which ensures that the names of the fallen are kept to the forefront of the memory of those who visit the cemeteries and memorials. I am sure that their work is appreciated by all visitors and who knows, I should like to think, even by those whose graves they tend. I think this is what Paul was driving at in "Flowers", but he is also troubled as he reflects that the same standards may not be evident in the Homeland, as he suggests in "Memorial".

His last poem, "Legacy", is an angry message to us all and portrays Paul's real sense of frustration at the senseless waste of life in evidence on the Somme and throughout the Western Front. Not happy with this, we repeated the process 21 years later and are still engaged in various theatres of war throughout the world. Is it any wonder then, that Paul, reflecting as he does through his poetry on the senselessness and futility of war, is angry that lessons from the past have not been learnt?

ACKNOWLEDGEMENTS

Our journey through these fields is over and I thank you for your company. My journey through this book started some two years ago and, as with all journeys, it has been made more enjoyable by my companions. My special thanks go to:

Professor Carl Chinn for being there, at the beginning, many years ago when I first started writing poetry and whose constant support gave me the confidence to begin this particular journey.

Donna Roberts, who like Carl, has been there since the beginning, but who, unlike Carl, has had the problem of deciphering my writing, unravelling my thoughts and, most difficult of all, following my ambiguous instructions. This book is a tribute to her success.

Terry Carter, who introduced me to the Somme area, and who, since then, has been my companion and guide on our visits and a good friend the rest of the time.

Lastly, it is fitting that the final person to be mentioned in this book is Elaine, my wife, for her unquestioning love and support on this book in particular and in all I do. She is my strength and it would never have been written without her.

Paul J Thornber
January 2006